Finding Refuge in the Ruins

DANIEL L. HARP

Book cover photo by Melissa L. Harp.
Back cover photo by Holden Photography.
Both are used by permission.
Book design by Christina Murdock

ISBN: 9798747374584
Independently published

DEDICATION

Dedicated to those who sacrificially adjusted their lives
to provide a network of love and support to me and
those most affected by my sin.

CONTENTS

FORWARD

If ever there was a testament to God's willingness and power to recover, restore, redeem, and reconcile us...this is it!

This is a story of recovery. All of us experience the reality of being lost, broken, and alienated. It is God who chases and finds us, mends our wounds, helps us heal, purifies us, becomes our peace, and assures us that we are His. Danny's story is an undeniable testimony illustrating how much God loves us, that we are never too far gone for His grace and mercy, and that life is completely His to give and sustain. His incredible story should provoke all of us to shift our perspective from seeing God's truth as something we should apply to our lives, to that which we should bring our lives into alignment with.

Scripture tells us to, "Know that the Lord is God. It is he who made us, and we are his; we are his people, the sheep of his pasture." (Psalm 100:3) God recovers those who are lost or stolen away because we belong to Him.

Finding Refuge in the Ruins invites you to journey with Danny from lost to found. He is living proof that there is nowhere we can lose ourselves that is too far and too dark that God cannot recover us. To be so completely lost physically, mentally, emotionally, and spiritually, Danny shares that hope can and does come from a God whose love is complete.

This is a story of restoration. We are reminded that "...the God of all grace, who called you to his eternal glory in Christ, after you have suffered a little while, will himself restore you and make you strong, firm, and steadfast." (First Peter 5:10)

I met Danny as he was experiencing the life restoration that only God can accomplish. I have spent my life hearing people's life stories where many times emphasis can easily be placed on the resiliency and perseverance of the human spirit, and how the love and support of others helped restore one to health. To this day, Danny's story remains the most incredible story I have ever heard, where all credit belongs to the Great Physician to restore.

This is a story of redemption. God has provided redemption from the overwhelming debt of our sinful nature and saved us from its due penalty. He encourages us within the pages of His Word that, "I have swept away your offenses like a cloud, your sins like the morning mist. Return to me, for I have redeemed you." (Isaiah 44:22)

We all love a great redemption story. Yet, the process of redemption often involves pain. Danny's physical redemption was very painful. His mental redemption was confusing and required faith that God's truth would renew his mind. His emotional redemption was a purging of fear, hurt and loss. His spiritual redemption involved dying to self and the mortification of sin that only the Spirit of God can fulfill once our spirit surrenders.

This is a story of reconciliation. God reconciles us to Himself, bringing harmony where there was chaos. It is a source of comfort in knowing, "For if, while we were God's enemies, we were reconciled to him through the death of his Son, how much more, having been reconciled, shall we be saved through his life!" (Romans 5:10)

While there is great peace that comes by knowing we are reconciled to God by grace through faith in Christ, we live here, in the flesh, with others who matter to us and whose lives have been affected by our life. Satisfyingly, Danny's story involves miraculous reconciliations with members of his family, many old and new friends, and a woman whose own life is a divinely crafted story.

I am so encouraged that Danny is sharing his story. What God has done for and through him is evidence that God's Word is true, that His love for us is beyond anything we can truly comprehend, and that we can trust Him with our lives completely.

Drew Ireland, LPCC
Cincinnati, Ohio

INTRODUCTION

I will not pretend that this is the story that was originally authored for my life. I will say that my story is one that is being used despite of my failures. Life has managed to take something broken and use it in a way that could not have possibly been imagined. I am sharing my story to encourage others who have lost their way. My hope is that they can rediscover their joy and purpose. Regret will not change my story, but my prayer is that it can provide hope for those who have found their journey rerouted by obstacles of their own making. Regardless of the level of difficulty of our path, we are not designed to be abandoned to walk it alone. We inherently long for companionship and a hand to hold as we make our way through moments of celebration and in the times when we face unimaginable pain.

My intent for the words I originally penned was not to publish a book but rather an exercise to reflect on the journey I have walked. During that journey, it became evident that my story could reveal the rawness of sin and the various needs within the lives of those it hurts. I was the grateful recipient of sincere mercy in my failures, and I also experienced pompous holiness among those who came cloaked as an ambassador of the church. If we are to provide genuine support to one another in times of hardship, may I suggest we find a balance of embracing an attitude of service while making sure it does not convey an attitude of arrogance to those on the outside looking in.

There is an urgent need for each of us to prepare ourselves to be approachable and sincere in every regard. An avenue for those who have lost their way to talk openly about their struggles without the fear of being judged, is a resource we must provide. A haven of retreat must be constructed for those who are broken. Judgment will come soon enough for all of us. God, rest assured, will take care of seeing that justice is done. He defined the role of judge as His responsibility within the stunning plan He has created for each of us to experience. He finds a unique balance of forgiveness, consequences, discipline, accountability, and unconditional love that He extends daily to each of us through His Son, Jesus Christ. Finding the balance that I speak of is all a part of what Christ depicted so wonderfully in His life and ministry.

Christ is the image of the balance that God wants each of us to observe and to know personally. Once we see what God is willing to do in our lives, the joy in sharing Him with others begins. His peace resting comfortably in our hearts is a treasure that He wants each of us to experience. He demonstrates His passion and concern for us throughout scripture. He communicates the blessings He wants us to enjoy. At times, we turn our back on His peace because it often must be coupled with changing something about ourselves that we enjoy or take pride in.

Do we understand that we are called as Christians and, corporately as a body of believers, to be a part of the forgiveness and redemption process in others' lives? Do we embrace the fact that God wants to use us in extending His peace to others? We must accept our calling in order to be the face of God for those who are struggling. The world needs a portrait of God, and it is our responsibility to demonstrate through our words and actions His character. God is compassionate, wise, forgiving, faithful, and merciful. Learning the discipline and significance of allowing God to serve others through us sits at the heart of transforming lives and allowing people to see His nature. While I certainly would not have chosen to see the church from the side that I have, and in the way that I did, it has given me a perspective of what it looks like from the outside looking in. I have seen a significant amount of good in people. I have also seen the worst in people when I simply needed to see Jesus.

I do not pretend to be perfect. I am a sinner. I am, however, unquestionably concerned about people. I have always been an individual who cares, especially for hurting people. People being mistreated or having their feelings hurt have always stirred something inside me to take a stand. I have always tried to advocate for those who are hurting and intentional to offer a word of encouragement or comfort. I have tried to carry a burden for those that others did not have time for or could not understand. That has been the most challenging part of my journey. My actions hurt others, and it brought about an incredibly unfair atmosphere. I hurt the people that I loved the most. I had been unfair to them. I paved a path of disaster, destroying the hearts that I cared for the most. Their experience of feeling afraid, shaken, and questioning everything they knew about me and the role I played within their lives, was something that I, sadly, generated. I became the reason for their pain. I was the arrow shot through their heart. My sin was playing out in my life and their life as well. This was the very thing I had warned others about for years. I knew God. I understood His might and His desire for us to be obedient. Did I think I would be the exception to His consequences?

I had it all. From the outside looking in, people saw an enviable life. I had a ministry that I enjoyed, responsibilities that gave me pleasure, a job that matched my skill set with a church that I loved. My home was a haven and a source of retreat from the everyday stresses of life and ministry. My life was a total package of what God had blessed me with daily.

My problem did not come from trying to escape the confines of God's instructions for my life or the stresses of my ministry. It came from something much more profound and personal. My problem was one that did not stem from an unhappy life or an unfulfilling profession. I loved both. The feelings that came with my sin were real and led me down a path that destroyed the life that God had blessed me in building.

My sin was not hidden from God. I knew that God could see my sin, and He knew from my heart-to-heart conversations with Him that I longed to step out of the dark hole that I had dug. In my inability or, perhaps, unwillingness to relinquish control, I created a world of isolation and loneliness. My deceived heart and mind convinced me that I had nowhere to turn. There was help available, and there were people who loved me. I could not see it because I was blinded by the darkness that sin had ushered into my life. I was scared. I was frightened. I could not see the other side of stepping out in faith, trusting God, and admitting to someone that I had a secret to share. I had seen what that had looked like for others. I had seen Christians, at times, be cruel, judgmental, and distant. I did not need that.

I needed help. Would the church be the church I knew God longed for them to be for a sinner like me? I wanted to believe they would, but unfortunately, in my tenure as a minister, I had been witness to numerous scenarios where the church had fallen so far from the model of providing Christ-like compassion and accountability for those who had fallen into sin. I had also seen, in many situations, the church be precisely what God had called them to be. Which scenario would play out for me? That was a question that I did not have an answer. It had hurt me at times, and I had seen it hurt others. My mistake was not trusting God.

JOURNAL - DAY ONE
The Journaling Begins

I have always felt a constant need to please people and to put them at ease in challenging situations and when dealing with difficult emotions. My desire to do so was not selfless. It gave me a sense of purpose and a bridle in which I could use to control the climate of emotions around me. I wanted to create an atmosphere of happiness. If tension were high, I stepped in providing a diversion. Contributing a distraction as people unknowingly stepped away from a difficult situation is what I did.

This practice did not allow me to develop the skill of coping with conflict and meeting the awkwardness of such circumstances with a proper and constructive response. As a young man, I never learned the art of being true to myself because of my constant self-imposed need to make people happy and maintain peace. Conflict, especially within the realm of relationships, made me anxious and uncomfortable. My experiences during my youth made it nearly impossible to know that there were healthy avenues to deal with and leverage such feelings. I could not find the right balance between having a genuine love for people and still holding firm to the path that I wanted to take or the words that I wanted to say. Nothing pleased me more than to set people at ease and to remove unpleasant feelings of contention, but in doing that, I would allow my emotional well to run dry. I did not realize that my longing to bring resolve for others was not for them at all. It was for me. It provided a semblance that everything was just as it should be and created a world that I could control. The process was complicated. It took creativity, time, and pretending to know others' thoughts and intentions. It became a pattern to suppress my strife. This behavior path was not sustainable emotionally, relationally, spiritually, or physically.

Exhausted and spent, I gave of myself recklessly to others with no thought of self-preservation, I continued down a toxic path, having convinced myself that giving oneself sacrificially was what all good followers of Christ did. After all, giving of oneself is a character of God. I failed to remember that God's expectation, more importantly, was for me to maintain myself spiritually. I was trying to be a warrior without the equipment I needed to fight and without the various pieces of armor in place. My heart became more and more pierced with the arrows of life and the feelings of defeat.

JOURNAL - DAY TWO
A Journal Entry

Growing exhausted from my battle, I tried to surround myself with positive and loving people. People became my fuel. I would pick and choose from each relationship what I thought I needed to function and maintain my happiness. I grew increasingly dependent on people. I managed to do that well for a time but found that they, too, are people. People are flawed, like me, and are often not capable of giving the joy that I was in search of finding. I was longing for something from people that only God could provide. I had placed my heart in the wrong hands. I had God's joy confused with happiness. This is something that I had passionately warned others about doing throughout my ministry. I know now why I was so passionate about people experiencing God's joy. I wanted desperately to understand and experience it myself. The practice of me explaining to others how they could obtain and maintain God's joy was easy. Putting it into practice for myself proved to be complicated.

JOURNAL - DAY THREE
A Journal Entry

As I continued to fail at protecting my own heart through the years, I became lonely. I was an enthusiastic soul, but my light was fading fast, and I did not dare let anyone know. Whatever the void was, I should have longed to fill that space with God. Unfortunately, I lacked the knowledge as a child and the discipline as an adult to do so. I believed in Him without hesitation, but I did not trust Him to be what I needed Him to be in my life. I searched for something right there in front of me, but I was looking for it in the wrong places. I was God's child. I was a son that He had created. His hands designed me with gifts that God, as my heavenly Father, was incredibly proud of. As a young boy, I was not able to see that truth. My sense of self-worth diminished, and my inability to see myself through the eyes of God grew. I was deceived, and in my ever-present desire to control what people thought about me, I learned the horrible habit of isolating myself and keeping my feelings tucked away, far from anyone to see. My young mind gave me poor advice as I sought approval from others. At the time, my advice was all I had to go on. Unfortunately, I tried to fill the void that I was experiencing emotionally. I took self and ill-advised measures to suppress my feelings of anxiety and uncertainty. Albeit seldom, this led to thoughts that I knew were not of God.

JOURNAL - DAY FOUR
A Journal Entry

As a young boy, I could often be found alone in the woods with my faithful dog, Judy. I would talk to her as if she were the only one in the world who could offer me words of advice. She provided me the unconditional love and acceptance that I wanted to experience. I loved that dog. She was a beautifully natured black Labrador Retriever that adored me and expected nothing in return, with only the exception of the occasional stick thrown for her to fetch. She would look deep into my eyes as if she understood every word I was saying. The woods adjacent to my childhood home in the country was my retreat from the world. It was where I could simply be me with no one to impress, disappoint or bother. While my family did not own the woods, I claimed them as my own. I knew every path, every stump and every tree in those woods. I enjoyed the wildlife, without fail, I would see on my adventures through what I had claimed as my kingdom.

As I isolated myself, I found places that I felt safe from the expectations of what others thought I should be. Sadly, I created a world that I kept hidden from others. I never learned the art of effectively sharing my heart and venting my feelings. This behavior created a cycle of frustration of pulling myself further and further away from people and circumstances that could have potentially filled the void of love and acceptance that I was looking for. I see that now. As a young man, I did not.

Grabbing my fishing pole and making my way to the pond to fish after school was another spot where I would find peace and a haven from a world that did not hurt. I enjoyed riding my dirt bike. I rode quite often throughout the countryside and back roads with the other boys who lived nearby, but it was riding alone that I enjoyed the most. I remember riding and thinking through problems that seemed monumental at the time.

I was intentional in filling my life with distractions that kept me occupied with something other than the loneliness I was experiencing, and I carried that practice into adulthood. Being lonely was what I hated the most, but isolation was the prescription I had written to deal with the emptiness. One was feeding the other, and I did not see how the two were constructing a grand stage for failure.

My outgoing personality became a false proscenium for my pain to hide behind. The pain became a wound that needed to be treated. I will not go as far as to say that the pain was too much to handle, but my feelings became misplaced, and my heart was misguided toward a source of comfort that was laden with traps for a young man of my age. It was a laceration in the tapestry of my life that was an opened wound for Satan to take full advantage of to infect my mind with deception and malice. It would materialize into something unimaginable for me and for many who would observe my eventual fall from the pulpit.

JOURNAL - DAY FIVE
A Journal Entry

At a young age, I discovered that I enjoyed singing. Singing was something that I often did to escape the boundaries of reality. Singing allowed me to exercise imagination as I slipped in and out of being the artist I was trying to emulate or the world in which the song was speaking. It took me away to a place where the cares and worries of life did not exist and it was something, I could do with absolutely no preparation or equipment. All I needed was me. As a child, it was rare for me not to have a tune or a song coming out of my mouth. If it was not coming out of my mouth, you could rest assured that I had a song in my heart. As I entered middle school, I had opportunities to sing with choirs and participate in community theatre productions. People started taking note of my voice and would tell me that I had a gift. Having been brought up in the church, I knew that, if given a gift, it needed to be used for God, which is exactly what I did. As invitations came for me to sing, I chose to sing songs that had an inspirational message of hope and love. Singing in church was something I regularly did.

Singing also became my avenue to God. More than being in church or praying, singing became a clear path to communicate my heart to God. It was the tool I used when I wanted an audience with God and when I needed to connect with Him personally. I thoroughly enjoyed singing and, to this day, embrace the art form as it serves me as a venue where God and I can meet as one.

Singing became more and more of a ministry in high school as I accepted invitations to sing, and with that came the idea of getting my college education at a Bible college. It was proposed to me by a friend that I send an audition tape to Johnson Bible College (now known as Johnson University) for a group of singers and musicians that were being put together to tour for a few weeks during the summer of 1985. This was the summer following my graduation from high school. I put my application and audition tape in the mail. A few weeks later, I learned that I was selected to tour with the group that summer. I made plans to make the trip to just east of Knoxville, Tennessee, to Johnson University.

Johnson University felt like home the moment I stepped foot on campus. It was a comfortable environment that sat beautifully in the rolling foothills of the Smoky Mountains. I knew immediately that Johnson University was a place I wanted to be, and it was a place to belong. The first evening we spent on campus, the director sat us all down, and we listened to the music that was selected for our summer tour. One song caught my attention, "Jesus is the King!" This song was upbeat, had a great instrumental accompaniment, and I knew that it would be the song, no doubt, that would get the attention of those who came to hear our concerts. It was a powerful song in so many regards, and it was apparent to me that it was a solo to be performed by a male tenor. I was going to make sure that the tenor singing that solo was me.

We worked our way through the concert material, rehearsing each song to perfection. When the day came to rehearse "Jesus is the King", the director asked who was interested in singing the solo. Several of us expressed interest, and the auditions for that solo began. One by one, the director listened to those interested in singing the solo. I confidently sang through the number and waited for his decision. The solo was given to me.

I arrogantly embraced the song and performed it nightly as we toured. It was a favorite among the other songs that we performed. On one occasion, the minister stepped to the pulpit following the concert, turned to our director, and said, "Before you leave, we want the little guy with the big mouth to sing that song again." The audience roared with applause and laughter, and I knew that I was getting the attention that I wanted in my young and immature heart. There were many nights that we performed it as an encore. With very little thought to the song's lyrics and meaning, I became attracted to the applause and attention that the song was getting for me. Conceitedly, I used the song as a tool to get my voice and name into the hearts and minds of the audience.

After our summer tour, we made our way back to Knoxville with plans of doing a farewell concert for family, friends, the Johnson University campus and the community of Knoxville. Our farewell concert would be our largest crowd yet. We were filled with the excitement of knowing that we had produced a successful tour. We were happy to reunite with our families but knew that our time together had ended. The concert would be bittersweet.

Told that we would be performing my song last that evening, I looked forward to it with great anticipation. When it came time for me to sing my solo, I stepped up to the microphone, placed it in my hand, took a deep breath, and waited for the instruments to start the accompaniment. With an ensemble of talented vocalists to back me up, I began to sing. That night, and this is hard for me to admit, for the first time, I listened to the words as I sang. I listened to what was at the core of the message. "He is alive, He is alive, my Lord is alive! Jesus is the King!" As I listened to the words, the message began to penetrate my heart in a way that I had never experienced before.

This song was not about me at all. It was about a Savior, a King, a Lord…My Lord! As the music unfolded and we moved closer and closer to the key change and the closing chorus, the message became more powerful and prominent. I needed to make Him King and Lord of my life! My heart was taken over with emotions, and my voice became still. With a lump in my throat that made it impossible to sing and with my eyes filled with tears, I became mesmerized by the lyrics. The ensemble continued to sing, and the band played on without me. I lowered the mic, holding it at my waist, hung my head, and with that, I heard applause as I had never heard applause before. It was something glorious. It was the sound of an audience knowing that something greater was taking place during that song than the song itself. It had touched a life. It had touched my life. With that, the crowd came to their feet with a thunderous standing ovation, and it was then that I realized that the applause and positive comments I had been getting all along were not about me after all. They were about a message of hope and the story of a resurrected Savior. At that moment, God spoke and told me that my voice and music needed to be for His glory and bringing Him honor and taking His message to a world that needed to hear His plan of salvation for their lives. It was also at that moment that my heart chose full-time Christian ministry. I set in motion a plan to attend Johnson University that fall.

My time at Johnson University was of great value. The experience allowed me to learn so much educationally and spiritually. The circle of friends I made in college are still close friends to this day and serve me as a source of encouragement. The institution, grounded in tradition and Biblical values, refined and prepared me for ministry.

My time in college afforded me ample opportunities to travel throughout the United States and in several foreign countries representing Johnson University and Christ, singing in churches, camps, conferences and building bridges with alumni and friends of the University. I will forever be grateful for my time and for the wonderful, caring family that I experienced while attending there.

CHAPTER ONE
The Snarl of Sin

After receiving my undergraduate degree, I served for nearly twenty-four years in full-time Christian Ministry. I loved it! My first ministry out of college focused on children and teenagers. The countless hours of planning and preparation were typically rewarded with the joy that I found in seeing my youth group members grow in their relationships with one another and with God. I was blessed tremendously through the years with many others who partnered with me in implementing successful programs for the children and youth that we served. Wanting a change of pace and an opportunity to grow in my ministry experience, I eventually served in Christian education, church assimilation, and leadership development. My years in full-time ministry were an endless collection of mission trips, conferences, ministry programs, church camps, and providing direction with curriculum and Christian education programs for children, youth, and adults. The personal touches that I had throughout my ministry years give me the most excellent satisfaction. I experienced so much laughter, so many tears, and numerous reasons to celebrate as I had the privilege of being a part of so many lives. I enjoyed every facet of serving within the church. I was passionate and sincere in what I did, and my years in ministry gave me a collection of cherished memories and experiences that I will remember and treasure forever. While it was, at times, exhausting and demanding, ministry was something that I thoroughly enjoyed. However, a trap had been set for me, and in my inattentiveness to my spiritual well-being, I would find myself torn between two worlds that were competing for my attention.

I continued to battle through my need to belong. I chose isolation over seeking the help that I needed. Seeking help would mean having to talk to someone and making myself vulnerable. At times, I had learned that the church could be judgmental and cruel. I needed a safe place and a trusted person who would hear my story, but Satan tricked me into thinking that no such place or person existed. Who would be kind enough to listen and afford me their time? I had talked myself so far into a dark hole that I did not feel worthy of someone's time or attention. I did not dare share my thoughts and struggles. It was best to keep them in the dark world that I had created. The darkness frightened me. Not only was the place I had made dark, but it clouded my judgment and understanding regarding every aspect of my life. It was a constant distraction as I aimlessly tried to find some source of light on my own. I must have given Satan a great deal of satisfaction as I chose to stay in the darkness. I was too frightened and proud to step into the light and unveil my need for help.

I stumbled into a world that materialized into something deplorable and incomprehensible. I failed to keep my spiritual armor in place. I was caught off guard. I fell. My sin had now gone beyond thoughts. It had become physical. A door was opened for me to participate in an act that would change my life forever. I allowed Satan to get the best of me and I took advantage of an opportunity that presented itself. I now had a far greater secret than the secrets confined within my heart and mind. I had a secret that had touched me physically.

My sin was not so much an action that was physically played out, but rather feelings and emotions that were placing shackles around my mind making it impossible to live with myself. No one could see the fear and anxiety that I was experiencing. The sin had a powerful grip on me, creating a pressure that was too hard for me to escape. The sin beat me down. There was an on-going need to suppress the complicated web of emotions that played out daily. The darkness became too dense. It was a vicious cycle that is difficult to understand until you experience it. It is terrifying to be controlled by something you hate. I was convinced that I was unable to avoid it.

My remorse and regret were as much a part of the secret I was keeping as the physical sin itself. I was carrying that too, alone. Trying to hold myself together was exhausting. I just wanted to be what everyone expected and needed me to be. I, too, had the same expectation for myself, but I could not find the combination I needed to unshackle the chains that paralyzed me emotionally.

Nobody could tell anything was wrong in that my heart was impossible to view. I cannot blame anyone for not recognizing that there was a problem eating away at my heart and mind. I had too many veils in place covering the parts of my heart that I did not want myself or others to see. It was too upsetting. There were portions of my heart that were hurting profoundly. My own feelings became foreign even to me and I found them to be impossible to define. As I pushed the hurt aside, I covered up each, one by one, which only made matters worse. I tried to rely on myself in finding the answers I was searching for. With each cover, I put in place, as I tried to function and cope, I made a mess that was getting more and more difficult for me to manage emotionally. The mask needed to be removed, and my heart needed to be dealt with in a way that would lead my feeble soul back to the pure and original state God had intended for me at birth, but much like a bandage that is too painful to remove, my misguided mind chose to leave the veil in place. My heart, the pure nature God originally placed within me, was now a sea of torment and deception.

I clung to God's hand tighter with each passing day. Kneeling, I would cry as I prayed for God to free me from the pain and torment of the sin that I had committed. I was so disappointed in myself and terrified of the thought that I had given Satan a victory. My relationship with God was real. I had always loved Him. I prayed constantly but did not fully understand the importance of being still and listening. As I look back, there is no doubt that God was instructing and guiding me, but my heart was too distracted and busy to listen. I was passionate about Him. However, I found that loving and fully trusting Him are two different things. At times, I thought He was all I had. I still refused to let people get a glimpse of what I felt. He heard my cries for help, witnessed the torment within my heart, and saw the tears I hid from others. I was sincere in my preaching and teaching and meant everything I said. I enthusiastically proclaimed His Word and rejoiced in others claiming Him as their Lord and King. For me, to surrender to Him meant trusting Him fully. To seek help would mean that I would have to trust people to be a part of my healing, steps forward, and redemption path. But trusting people was a step I could not take. My words to others were now falling into conflict with my inability to trust and obey.

I had been conditioned not to trust people. I had been exposed to all kinds of people in life and ministry. Too many of them had let me down and had used me for something they wanted in return. A few situations within my first ministry were, indeed, emotionally abusive. My behavior of protecting my heart and keeping it from being vulnerable to others' careless and thoughtless words was reinforced.

I had learned from my extensive experience as a shepherd within the church that sheep bite and that they can bite hard. The biting was typically done all in the name of the Lord, of course.

At the core of my struggle was my inability to trust God and allowing Him to teach me to deal with the disappointment and heartbreak that people can often bring into our lives. In the long run, people did let me down. God, of course, knew this truth all along, and I know now that this is why He enthusiastically and consistently instructs us to trust Him. I had proved myself wrong in thinking that I needed more than God's love. The great and glorious truth revealed in my struggle is that God is all that matters. Having God and only God is enough. I should have seen this truth from the beginning. He was enough. Unfortunately, for me, it took God holding me firmly by the shoulders and shaking me like the child that I am for me to understand all that He wanted to be for me and my life. He was all I ever needed. I know that now.

CHAPTER TWO
Being Sick and the Phone Call

The unexpected came at the age of forty-four and in my twenty-fourth year of full-time ministry. I had always been healthy. Full of energy, my life was an enthusiastic, animated journey. As I look back, there were signs that something physically was not quite right, but I mistook many of the symptoms I was experiencing as signs that I was getting older. Within a relatively short period of time, I started experiencing symptoms that were not going away. I dealt with fatigue, fever, and loss of appetite and weight. With the symptoms now lasting for more than three months, I knew in my heart that something was not right and that it was far more than simply getting older. Relatives and friends were starting to comment on my weight loss. "You look great!" they would say with no way of knowing that my unplanned weight loss had become of great concern to me. I had some extra weight to lose, and, for a time, I did not mind shedding a few pounds. Suspecting cancer, I grew paranoid and started weighing myself daily. Each week I would lose another three or four pounds. Over the course of about four weeks, I grew increasingly weak and frail. I kept telling myself that I would go to the doctor after the holidays. I wrote it off as an intestinal issue and had even placed myself on some probiotics, thinking that, with time, the physical problems I was having would go away.

Just after the holidays, I woke up with a rash all over my body and knew that I needed to see my doctor immediately. My doctor diagnosed it as an allergic reaction to something that I had come in contact with and prescribed an antihistamine. The rash went away within a day or so.

The following Sunday evening, after preaching, I ran a high fever and could barely find the energy to walk. I decided to go to an urgent care facility. My doctor examined me thoroughly and knew that something did not add up. After a series of questions, he scheduled me for a blood test. He also asked me specifically if I had been exposed to HIV. My response was an immediate "No." As he talked more about my symptoms and as my mind reflected on what I had done years earlier, I wondered if my sin was not coming back to bite me and bite me hard. Surely an isolated situation would not have left me with the unspeakable consequence of HIV. Leaving the urgent care facility and knowing the conversations that needed to follow was nothing short of a nightmare. It was impossible for me to sort through all that I was thinking and feeling. While I waited on the results, I knew that I needed to tell my family that I had done something years earlier that could have possibly exposed me to the deadly virus. If I had been exposed, I did not know it. Given what I had done and the doctor's question about possible exposure, I knew that the possibility, albeit slim, was there. I was terrified. Where would I start, and what could I possibly say so my story would make sense to my family or to anyone for that matter. I had the painful task of telling my family that there was a possibility of the HIV test coming back positive. I could not help but wonder if my moment of indiscretion years earlier would become a death sentence.

The four days while waiting on my test results were unimaginable. I called my parents to my home and attempted to tell them what was going on. Regardless of what the results of my blood work would reveal, my family needed to know that I was sick and growing weaker with every passing day. I remember lying initially as to how the virus was contracted. I was terrified and confused. Where could this conversation possibly begin? There were no excuses for what I had done, and I knew the reasons were irrelevant given the severe nature of the circumstances unfolding. Would the truth of what I had done sever my relationship with those I cared about the most? How could I possibly find the words to tell them that I had put my health and family in jeopardy? I was desperate. There was so much at stake. The emotions were far too great for me to get a handle on what was happening. I needed time to figure things out, but time was not on my side. I was very sick, and my family deserved answers immediately. My world as I knew it was crumbling quickly. The terrifying climate of what I have just described is all I remember. As I try to look back, those last few days at home are a blur. I have little memory of that time. My physical and mental state was deteriorating quickly. It was challenging to focus. To this day, if there is one thing that haunts me the most, it is the fact that I could not find the words or gather the emotions and courage I needed to craft the thoughts and conversation that everyone involved rightly deserved. Of course, now, I know why I could not do so. I would later learn that it was fungal meningitis that was playing havoc on my brain.

My ability to reason and understand the days leading up to my hospitalization was minimal. Had I known then what I know now, I would have waited to have those difficult conversations until I was more mentally and physically able to do so. I am not suggesting that those in my life did not deserve answers then, but what I do regret is not being able to articulate the answers, they deserved. I had no time to process the information for myself and was asked to process it and make sense of it for others. Cognitively, with the undiagnosed meningitis, there was little I was able to process for them or me.

Getting a personal phone call at home from your family physician is not something that happens often. So, when I received such a call, I knew that something was seriously wrong. I had tested positive for HIV.

With the confirmation that I had HIV, I asked the elders of the church where I was serving to come to my home and I voluntarily resigned from my ministry. I did not tell them about my diagnosis. I told them I needed to resign immediately due to having made a decision that had put my marriage and health in jeopardy. I had made decisions that were not becoming of a man that God had called to lead a church. I had sinned and needed to heal emotionally. I could not possibly lead others spiritually. I thought I was dying. Leaving the ministry meant I would not have an income, and that was one more worry to add to my jumbled thoughts and the unfolding crisis. Undoubtedly, this was of great concern for others that my situation was touching. As I recall, stepping down from my ministry was the only thing that was clear in my mind regarding the steps that I needed to take.

It was quite clear that I would have to lean on my faith in God more than ever. I had preached to others about the importance of trusting God in times of trials, and I would need to put this truth into action. I questioned if I had ever trusted Him fully. He was all I had then, and I would find that He was all I would need.

A few days after getting the phone call with the HIV diagnosis and resigning from my church position, I collapsed in the bathroom. An ambulance was called. I pled with my family not to send me away. As sick as I was, I was quite sure that I would not live to see my home or family again. As I was placed on a stretcher and rolled to the ambulance sitting in the driveway, I looked back and saw my house and sensed that I would never see my home again. I never did. The terror of that moment is still so vivid in my mind. I was transported to the local hospital, where doctors quickly determined that I needed to be moved to a larger and more equipped hospital. My medical condition was far too severe for the local hospital to handle.

CHAPTER THREE
Reactions and a Hospital Stay

The decision was made to transport me to The Ohio State Wexner Medical Center in Columbus, Ohio. With my immune system damaged and weak, doctors determined that I had contracted fungal meningitis. Slow-growing meningitis had taken advantage of my damaged immune system and was the cause of my sickness. The rare form of meningitis caused fluid on my brain and spinal cord. The pressure of that fluid was putting my life in danger. The hospital also ran tests to determine the levels of my HIV viral load and to determine the condition of my now compromised immune system. Fortunately, I was in the care of one of the best teams of infectious disease doctors in the country. The doctors believed I had picked up meningitis from my small backyard flock of chickens. My small flock was a hobby that I had enjoyed. I kept my coop clean, but with my immune system compromised, fungal meningitis took the opportunity to attack.

Doctors made the meningitis treatment their priority and told my family that my HIV viral load was "off the charts" and that significant damage to my immune system had already occurred. With the HIV viral load being what it was and my immune system being severely damaged, my doctors made their diagnosis. The diagnosis was full-blown Acquired Immune Deficiency Syndrome (AIDS). The treatment for my AIDS would have to wait as the team of doctors focused on treating the fungal meningitis and trying to save my life.

My one hundred-and fifty-five-pound body withered away to one hundred and fifteen pounds. The excess fluid on my brain and spine needed drained. My muscle tone completely disappeared. It took all the strength I had to hold my head up. For several days I had a tough time comprehending where I was and the severity of my situation. I knew I was in a hospital, but I was confused, disoriented, and frustrated. I longed to see familiar faces. I had no sense of time and no ability to determine what was going on around me.

There was not one facet of my situation I could control. I was trapped in my weakened state and held captive by a sin that came with horrific consequences. My choice was to either surrender my life to God or fight. I was too tired to fight. By default, I surrendered angrily and with reservation to God. I did not care. I wanted out of my bed and out of my room. I wanted to go home to die in an environment that was familiar and comfortable. I wanted someone to hold my hand. I did not want to die alone and certainly not like this. I could not imagine getting better given my critical state, but I also had no desire to get better. I was tired, and my mind had concluded that getting better would mean having to face the life that I had single-handedly destroyed. The thought of having to take responsibility for the damage I had caused was overwhelming. I resolved that dying would be much easier.

After many attempts to get out of my bed, I was eventually strapped down and put on "watch," which means the hospital placed someone in my room to keep an eye on me around the clock. I was scared, alone, and ashamed. Nothing made sense to me. I did not understand what was going on around me. I could hear voices but very seldom understood what people were saying. There were times I could sense someone was in the room, but for whatever reason, they chose not to speak. My treatment involved what seemed to be daily spinal taps, blood being drawn, and a constant state of being poked and prodded by those caring for me. I simply laid there like a rag doll doing and giving them whatever they wanted. I was too sick to care. The hate that filled my heart was raw and real. It was a hate for what I had done. I knew better! I had preached about consequences throughout my entire ministry. Why did I think I was going to be the exception? I developed deep hate for the person I had allowed myself to become.

I lost the ability to control my bowels and bladder, and there were several nights that I slept in my own mess, given my inability to communicate to my nurse that I needed assistance. I prayed to God that He would take my life. I could not tolerate the loneliness I was experiencing. In the hospital's darkness and unfamiliar surroundings, I was physically isolated. Having given up on my spiritual and emotional well-being, the void of what I was feeling was, in my mind, impossible to escape. I wanted to die. Eventually, within a few days, the meningitis, took me in and out of consciousness. There is a period of my hospitalization that I am unable to recall.

I believe it was on day 4 or 5 of my hospitalization that I could determine that something was not quite right with my vision. My eyesight was quickly deteriorating, and I lost the ability to make out faces. I could hear voices, but I was unable to respond. Within a few days, I lost my eyesight completely. I now had the frustration of wondering if I was blind, in a very dark room or if I had perhaps died. Did my doctors know I was blind? I did not have the ability to tell them, and I did not even know what I was experiencing. Again, cognitively, I was not able to function. I lost the ability to put my thoughts into words and, if words came, I could not put them into a logical order for them to make sense to anyone who was listening.

Eating a meal had become a time-consuming chore filled with tears, anger, and frustration. I remember a nurse bringing my food and leaving it on the table in front of me. It was only from sensing the nurse's presence and smelling the food that I even knew a meal was in front of me at all. I hesitated to dive in, thinking that the nurse would return to assist me or feed me. I could not see my tray or the food. It was evident that I was expected to eat without help. Trying to remain positive and calm, I felt my way across the tray with my fingertips, looking for a fork, knife, or spoon. I tried to determine what was on the tray by feeling the food. I sobbed. I felt so pathetic at that moment. I remember being so angry at God and myself. I wanted and needed help at that moment. I had only myself to blame, but was I being foolish and unreasonable to think that I deserved support and encouragement in this uncharted portion of my life? Was my need for emotional help unreasonable, and was it in line with the consequences I was facing? I was trying to maneuver through the meal the best that I could.

Was this the foreshadowing of the church's reaction to a sinner? Would I be left to fend for myself? I had no idea what my future held.

I was uncertain about what was in front of me as far as food and how I was to manage eating it. I tried. I really tried, but I couldn't. Outside of eating with my fingers, I had no idea how to eat with dignity, not to mention manners. I angrily yelled a couple of expletives out of frustration, not realizing the nurse was still in the room. At that moment, the thought actually and, very clearly, crossed my mind to throw the tray. Perhaps that would get someone's attention. The nurse, who I did not realize was still in the room, came over to me, sternly put the fork in my hand, opened my carton of milk, told me what was on my tray, and told me to stop feeling sorry for myself. I cried. I thought to myself how insensitive he was to me and my situation.

I wanted pity. He gave me harsh words. I wanted help. He gave me instructions as to how I could help myself. I was filled with hate for this nurse. I hated him, my situation, myself, and God. There was not one thing in that moment I could embrace as being positive in my life. As I sat in darkness, I pondered ways to take my own life so that I could put myself and those that had been saddled with my care out of their misery.

Ironically, I later learned my nurse was also living with HIV and had been doing so for years. His actions were reflective of his concern for me and in his determination to help me to be able to accept my new reality...my reality of living with AIDS. He was doing me a favor in telling me, in so many words, to deal with it and to get over myself. There was so much I had taken for granted up to this point in my life. I had not appreciated the treasure of having good health. I could not imagine ever being able to take care of myself again or having the freedom of being independent. While unaware of it at the time, I was not too far from understanding my situation's reality. Eventually, I would learn that during my hospitalization, my family was told to make arrangements for me to go to a nursing home should I be released from the hospital at all. Doctors were not confident that I could take care of myself and felt that a nursing home facility would be the best option for my family and me.

One afternoon an eye doctor came into my room to do an eye examination. My mom and dad were there. The doctor asked me to read the cards in front of my face. I requested that the lights in my room be turned on before we began the eye test because it was too dark for me to see anything. The doctor told me that the lights were already on. I then asked my mother to open the blinds to let additional light into the room. They told me the blinds were opened. I knew at that moment, as did everyone else in the room, that I was blind. The reality of that moment was more than I could absorb. My emotions were a mix of devastation and terror. I wondered if I would ever see again.

Oddly, my coping mechanism was in convincing myself that I was dying. The thought of dying gave me peace. In death, I would be free from the diagnosis, the symptoms and ultimately the consequences of living with AIDS. For everyone else, it was business as usual. My meningitis had to be treated. I had no option. I was trapped in that hospital bed whether I wanted to get better or not. I knew that the darkness I had been experiencing was blindness and not just a symptom of my confused and unstable mental state.

In the darkness of blindness, I imagined my surroundings and tried to, in my mind, create a portrait of my caregivers based on voices and mannerisms. I could only hear their voices and feel the touch of their hands as they examined me. The   medical team that assembled to make their plan for my recovery was in and out of my room numerous times daily. They were making assessments on my condition and ordering the various scans, tests and evaluations to give them the information they needed regarding my situation. Their presence in my room was usually followed by another revelation about how critical I had become. As much as I hated to sense a doctor's presence in my room, it was better than the silence that I learned to despise more and more as each day passed. My hospital room was a stale, cold, and frightening environment. I am sure it would not have been quite as scary had I not been blind, and my diagnosis not been so terrifying.

My entire hospital stay was hell. Ashamed, lonely, afraid, and physically incapacitated, I waited with not knowing what I was waiting for. I had to lie on my side due to the tube inserted in my back to drain the fluid. My body hurt. My heart hurt. When I was awake, I longed to hear a friend or family member's familiar voice. Most of the voices I heard were not familiar at all. They were doctors and medical students who were there to examine me and make a diagnosis and decision on their next course of action to help me take my steps towards recovery. I always found it interesting that they talked to one another and my parents as if I were not in the room. At times I could hear the doctors ask my parents to step into the hallway to discuss my condition.

I was in the dark in more ways than one. I was in the dark about my physical condition's actual state, and I grew increasingly concerned about every facet of my life. People were making long-term decisions for me, assuming that my life was over. For some within the church, perhaps, the determination had been made that I would die. I thought my life was over as well. If everyone had so quickly written me out of their life and had immediately jumped to the conclusion that I was going to die, how would those same people deal with me making a recovery? Would my recovery only mean more pain and disappointment for them, or would it give people a change of heart in seeing that God was much bigger than the situation all of us were currently walking through?

The next several days were filled with me asking to see family and friends. My numerous requests were met with a silence which only added to my torment and frustration. Were they not allowed to see me? Was I contagious? I longed for someone to explain to me what was happening. On my own, I was to determine how others were reacting to my diagnosis and my sin. Had my friends and others chosen to step out of my life? If so, I had no opportunity to ask for forgiveness or say goodbye.

CHAPTER FOUR
An Appeal and Voices of Encouragement

One afternoon, my mother held my hand and told me that she and dad needed to leave the hospital, assuring me that they would be back the next day. They were tired, and things at their home, an hour away, needed attention. They had visited me daily, sitting for hours in my room, hoping to get the latest report from my doctors' team. They, too, were dealing with the uncertainty and humiliation of my illness. Their forty-four-year-old son and self-professed man of God was now dying in a hospital bed with AIDS. How would they explain that to their card club, golf buddies, extended family, and church? They had a great deal to sort out.

I did not want to be left alone and begged them to stay. In tears, I asked them to please call someone from my church to come and sit with me. While my mom hesitated to do so, she finally asked me for a list of people she could call. The list I gave her was a list of friends, church staff members, and my Bible study group. The names that I passed along to my mom were people I considered family. I begged her to make the phone calls to see if anyone was willing to come and sit with me through the night. I was confident that someone would come. My mom's phone calls and requests for help that evening were met with numerous excuses as to why people could not come and sit with me. I could tell from the tone of her voice, as she talked on the phone, that things were not going well, and the reality of what the church thought of me was becoming more and more transparent. I was frightened. I was terrified of being left alone in the physical and spiritual darkness I had created. If the church did not care, who would? Understanding how frightened I was and knowing that my parents needed to get some rest, my sister made the trip to sit with me that night.

Dixie, my youngest sister, sat with me in the hospital that night, holding my hand. That is all I needed. I simply needed someone to hold my hand and assure me that I was not alone. Knowing that I was frightened by the room's silence and darkness, she kept talking. She shared memories of our childhood. She talked about our grandparents and the fond memories that each of us had spending weekends in the small town of Lynchburg, Ohio. She spoke about Grandma Shoop's chickens and goats, and she talked about the swing that Grandpa Hendee had hung for us from the old sycamore tree in their front yard. She asked if I remembered Sport, my grandparent's Dalmatian. As children, we convinced ourselves that Sport knew how to play hide and seek. She recalled the various food and treats that were always readily available when we would visit our grandparents…treats that were only available at our parent's home on special occasions. She had the monumental task of taking my mind off the situation at hand. She wanted to bring me some peace that evening, and she put her schedule, her family, and job aside to be used by God.

As Dixie fed me pudding and ice cream throughout the night, she kept my thoughts on pleasant memories. The memories that she recalled for both of us focused my mind on who I was and the people who would expect me to press on and carry out a legacy of dignity and positive thinking in this very dark time. She painted a picture of my life and reminded me of all the good that was still very much a part of who I was and who God wanted me to be. I remember her making me laugh that night. Laughing, up to that point, was not something I ever thought I would do again. There was a great deal of crying that night, but it was laughter that was speaking to my hurting heart and served as healing as we shared in what has now become my fondest memory of time spent with my sister, Dixie. My little sister…my crazy, wacky little sister, was used that night to be God's face, His voice, and His ear in my time of need. A hand to hold, an encouraging word, and an ear to listen were all I needed that night. The ministry she provided, when others would not, put my heart and mind at ease. If only for a few hours, she gave me a peace that Christ wants each of us to experience when the circumstances in our lives become more than we can handle by ourselves. I found rest that night and a safe refuge I could trust.

Whoever dwells in the shelter of the Most High will rest in the shadow of the Almighty. I will say of the Lord, "He is my refuge and my fortress, my God, in whom I trust."
Psalms 91:1-2

There were a few people who came to visit during my hospital stay. I do not mean to negate their visits and concern, but my ability to think and have conversations with them was limited. I was trying hard to digest what was going on in my life. I needed someone to help me understand the reality of my situation. That was the conversation I needed someone to have with me. If anyone did engage me in a conversation in those first few weeks of my diagnosis, it was in their effort to help them understand what I had done. I did not understand it myself. I did not have the wherewithal to talk about it. I needed time to ponder what it meant for my family and me. While my doctor knew the importance of me needing time to absorb what was going on, my family and friends, unfortunately, did not. There was no outlet provided for me in the first several weeks to talk openly about the things I needed to sort out. I was left alone to figure things out on my own. I created a misguided and unimaginable diagnosis for my life as I pressed forward in trying to get a plan for my life physically and emotionally. That scenario made matters worse. My mind raced with no opportunity to rest and settle for the moments that God needed to speak to my heart.

While dealing with the idea of having AIDS, the only thing I felt with certainty was a sense of liberation and peace. I knew the damage had already been done by the time my struggle was public, but I prayed that God would grant me the time to get my heart right with Him and salvage the part of me that had a chance to live for eternity…my soul. I could now get the help I wanted and needed, and I could do it without the weight of secrets, lies, and deception. I was free and placed in a position where I had to trust God. He was all I had. The small remnant of peace that I was experiencing was not something I shared with others during those first few weeks after my diagnosis. I knew that conversation needed to wait and would have been difficult for others to understand. Again, up to that point, no one seemed adequately equipped or interested in having that level of discussion with me.

Sadly, the meningitis deleted names, places, and pockets of time from my memory and robbed me of the ability to work within the realm of accurate timelines and reality. For those who did come and visit, I imagine that the sight of my physical condition was shocking. Most did not know what to say or what to do. It was difficult for everyone involved. There was no practice run or rehearsal for the situation we found ourselves living within. It happened so quickly and without warning. I know that some acquaintances made the trip to see me to get a first-hand glimpse at what others had described. I am confident that some came to visit to see the spectacle that was me with AIDS.

Many of the players, given the situation, dropped the ball (myself included). This was of no fault of our own. We were all walking in a land of circumstances that was new and foreign for each of us. God knows the limitations of our human hearts. For this reason, He calls on us to lean on Him, taking on a portion of His Spirit as we deal with difficult situations. With God's Spirit within our hearts and minds, it will be His words of encouragement and wisdom that prevails in those times when we are at a loss of what to say or do. It is not a weakness to depend on God. Relying on God in difficult times is a sign of strength, incredible courage, and discipline. It takes faith and trust. I wish that I and others had not traveled portions of my journey alone. We would have all been much better off to have relied on God to lead the way as we abandoned our limited thoughts and emotions toward a situation that was unfathomable for all of us.

There were small lights that God continued to place in my life. My attitude and mental state made them difficult to see, but there were small beacons of hope all around. Each morning the cleaning lady would come into my room. She was kind and always offered a word of encouragement. On most mornings, I knew she had entered my room due to the hymns that she sang softly as she went about her cleaning routine. Every morning, she asked me what I had eaten for breakfast as she was intentional in starting a conversation. She talked about her children. She never failed in mentioning how very blessed she was to have her job and made it a point to let me know that God had always provided for her and her family. As I look back, she made a commendable attempt to turn my heart toward the blessings that I was experiencing even in the ruins of my deep heartache.

Some nurses would also take time to sit and talk to me. They did what they could to provide me with the emotional support I needed. One nurse, in particular, was interested in taking a mission trip. Knowing that I was a former minister, asked me about the steps that she needed to take to make her goal of taking a mission trip a reality. I reminisced about the mission trips I had taken around the world.

It was refreshing to think about the lives that I had touched positively, and the conversation was a diversion from the constant thoughts of the lives I had hurt. Assuring me that I would heal, she was confident that I would one day have the opportunity to minister again. She spoke of God's grace and His mercy, and she was confident that

God was not finished with me yet. She spoke of His power and told me that He had a plan that He would reveal to me in time. She encouraged me to hold tight to His hand as He led me in the steps that He needed me to take toward redemption. I wanted to believe her, but it was difficult to imagine anything outside of that hospital room due to my situation casting a dark cloud over everything.

CHAPTER FIVE
Getting Back on My Feet

As my hospital stay progressed, doctors figured it was time to get me on my feet to see if I could walk. Not only was I going to need to learn to walk, but I would need to learn to walk as a blind man. I was hesitant even to try, but it was evident that refusing to try was not an option. I was encouraged to sit up in the bed. Sitting up was easier said than done. Not only was I weak, but I also had an IV in my arm and a drainage line coming out of my back that I had to be careful not to pull out. I had been flat for so long that sitting up was about all that I could handle. It was excruciatingly painful. My back had become so weak that holding my body in a sitting position was more than I could physically manage.

After getting me in a sitting position, I begged them to leave me alone. I was already exhausted, and I had not even started the process of trying to walk. The therapists asked me to turn and place my feet over the side of the bed as they prepared to get me up and on my feet for the first time in nearly two weeks. All I wanted was to be allowed to lie back down and rest. My words and tears could not convince them to leave me alone. My doctor had given them instructions to get me out of that bed, which is precisely what they were going to do. I felt a belt being wrapped around my waist. On each hip, attached to the belt, a clip was fastened to each therapist, one on each side. The two young men assisting me assured me that they would not let me fall or bump into anything. As I shifted my weight from the bed to my feet, the assistants spoke words of encouragement and instruction. I placed my weight on my legs and moved forward slowly. There were no steps. I could only shuffle my feet, unable to lift them off the floor. I remember being surprised and heartbroken about how wobbly my legs were, and I was reminded at that moment as to how sick and weak I was. Tethered to the IV pole and with the line still draining fluid from my back, I tried to progress forward toward the door of my room.

I had lost my ability to walk. My legs were so weak and would give out with no warning. It was like having the floor drop out from underneath me every three or four steps. I had to trust those that were now in charge of my care to hold me tight and not let me fall. I would compare the uneasy and unpredictable experience with that of sitting on a dunking machine and the feeling one gets while waiting for the ball to hit the target, dropping the seat quickly and unexpectedly out from under you.

Strapped to the two physical therapy assistants and with the assistance of a walker to lean on, I began the task of teaching myself how to walk again. Being blind, the endeavor of learning to walk again was overwhelming. How could they possibly expect me to take steps forward? What was there to take steps toward? Why was this circus of learning to walk again necessary at all? I did not have any plans of leaving the hospital alive. If I did, my life would be the life of being an invalid. I cried as I struggled to walk. These were the same robust, fast and muscular legs that had run the baton to the anchor in the relays that I had run in high school. These were the same intimidating legs that ran past my opponent as I sprinted toward the goalie in my soccer playing days. My legs had always been strong, steady, and quick to react to a strategically placed tennis ball sent into my side of the tennis court. Now, within a few weeks, they were worthless. There was no muscle tone, and how could I possibly be expected to walk or run again if I couldn't even find the strength to stand?

My pride became an issue. I wanted the young men who were helping me to have a glimpse of me just a few months earlier as I had orchestrated and coached a tennis camp for our community. I was an active, healthy, and physically strong man. That was the person that I wanted them to see at that moment. I did not want them to see the pathetic, small remnant of a man that was disintegrating physically in a hospital. The inability to see where I was going added to my sense of defeat. Being blind and learning to walk again would be far more complicated than I had thought. Again, I had only myself to blame. It was not from a car accident or a heroic war injury. It was AIDS. As I struggled down the hallway, it was challenging to think of anything other than what people thought as they witnessed my awkward attempt. I felt as if I were on display and being paraded down the hospital corridor for the sake of others to get a good glimpse of a life with AIDS.

My thoughts were extreme and, as I think back, ridiculous, but those thoughts crossed my mind that day and added to my sense of defeat.

In total darkness, I could hear voices, sensed the presence of people as they walked by, and felt the tight squeeze of the young men's hands around my arms. Their grip was so tight that it was painful. Still, ironically, assuring and comforting in that, as I recall, other than my sister holding my hand the night she attended me, it was some of the first physical touches I had experienced since being admitted to the hospital. I would need to trust those whose job it was to help me walk again.

Spiritually, I would need to do the same. I had to trust God. I had no clear direction spiritually. I could not see where my life was going from this point forward, and I could not see or imagine anything that looked like a finish line. In every aspect of my life, this process would be a marathon. It was going to take endurance. This process was not going to be an eleven-second burst of energy thrusting me to the finish line, and there was not going to be a teammate to complete the race for me. The anchor would have to be me if I finished this race at all. If I were going to reach the finish line with dignity and credibility, I would need a great deal of help. I would need to surrender to God and follow His instructions. This race would be a race that would last a lifetime, and I needed to prepare myself to run the distance. The question was, could I?

CHAPTER SIX
Speaking Truth and Finding Vision

I lost track of time. I could not have told you how long I had been in the hospital. My days and nights were one. They blended with no way for me to differentiate between the two. Being blind, it was dark twenty-four hours a day. I slept a great deal. Sleep was my only escape from reality. Awake, I would worry. The sounds that I heard routinely in my hospital room were tormenting. The alarm that would sound each time my IV bag needed replacing startled me every time. The hiss of my blood pressure cuff, which took my blood pressure every 30 minutes, agitated me as if it were purposefully trying to keep me from sleeping. The distant and annoying echo of the hospital intercom system announcing codes and making appeals for doctors was non-stop.

My mother's cell phone's ring tone was the most haunting and disturbing sound. Each time it would go off, she would leave the room, and I was sure she was talking to someone about my diagnosis. No doubt, some information was kept from me for my own good. Each time her cell phone rang, my heart would miss a beat, thinking that it was someone who may be calling to speak to me. My hopes would rise and then quickly fall as I heard my mom walk out of the room. I hated that ring tone. I associated it with my mother talking to people and making plans for me and my new life with AIDS. I was not consulted or included in any conversation regarding my future. I could only conclude that I had lost that privilege and, in my mind, rightfully so.

I remember a hospital visit from an elder from the church I served before my resignation. I am not sure if the other elders had asked him to visit me or if his visit, and eventual inquiry, was self-designated. He asked me what I wanted him and the other elders to tell the church. I told him to tell them the truth. He questioned the wisdom in telling the congregation the truth about my diagnosis. I recall telling him that the church needed the truth as a solid starting point to know how to minister to my family and me. Without knowing my resignation and my diagnosis, they would only become confused by my absence, and that people would start to fill in the blank with their imaginations. They needed a foundation of truth to build upon. They needed a door to walk through as they assembled themselves to deal with a situation far beyond anything imaginable. My situation was an opportunity to grow and an opportunity to exercise the power of God and for them to be the church that God calls us to be. It was also an opportunity for me to take a bold step in putting a stop to the pattern of deceit I had created in my attempt to hide the truth.

Jesus said, "If you hold to my teaching, you are my disciples. Then you will know the truth, and the truth will set you free.
John 8:31,32

I do not know if my wishes were honored. I asked for the truth to be shared. I no longer had to hide behind a lie. I could now deal openly with the demons I had faced. Not knowing what was being said and talked about among the jury of the church added to my collection of emotions. I grew paranoid and frightened. I knew conclusions were being formed, and decisions were being made. My life was out of my hands. I could not possibly control what others were saying. I did, however, know that if I spoke the truth moving forward, the truth would serve as an extinguisher of sorts to keep the fire of gossip and hearsay at bay. I did not want to be to matter of fact about what I had done, making a difficult situation even worse for the others who were suffering the consequences of my actions. I did, however, know that in moving forward, the truth would serve as a starting point for healing for everyone.

As I woke up from a nap that same afternoon, I could scarcely see a pattern as I turned my eyes toward the ceiling. I saw a design. I called the nurse, and I asked her to describe the ceiling. Her description matched what I was seeing. My eyesight was returning. Within a few days of that moment, I was able to see vague shadows and lights, but I was far from being able to recognize faces, see images on the television or read. Doctors could not say to what degree I would get my eyesight back. The ability to see the ceiling tiles' design was a small step forward that I could celebrate.

I was unsure if it was encouragement or a reward for good behavior, but my doctors eventually moved me to a room that overlooked the Ohio State Buckeye's "Shoe" ...the OSU football stadium. Being a fan and having had the opportunity to make the trip to Pasadena, California, to watch the Ohio State Buckeyes play in the Rose Bowl a year earlier, I suppose my doctors thought the view would be something that I would enjoy. I appreciated their gesture, but the move only served as a discouragement in that I could not see the grandeur of what was just outside my window. Doctors and my parents tried to describe the view, but I could only see shadows. My eyes could not see anything that looked like a stadium.

This inability to see what was right outside my window was a vivid illustration of my life. God was willing and able to love me through anything I placed at the foot of the cross, but Satan hid the view of what had always been within reach. I could not see the side of God that I could trust. For me, it was elusive. Maybe it is the side of God that we are not supposed to see clearly until we, in faith, step trustingly and follow Him fully. I had contemplated that step so often throughout my life, but my flawed human fear held me back. Faith in God has always been explained to me as believing in someone or something that we cannot see. I know the significance of what that means and how my faith in God is crucial to living a life as an obedient child of God. Just like the OSU football stadium, I knew it was real, but I had a hard time believing that it was just outside my window for me to view and enjoy. I had to trust that it was there.

As a believer, my spiritual eyes were not only fooled, but they were blinded. I had lost sight of the light that Christ is and that He is willing to shine in the hearts of those who believe.

The god of this age has blinded the minds of unbelievers so that they cannot see the light of the gospel that displays the glory of Christ, who is the image of God.

For what we preach is not ourselves, but Jesus Christ as Lord, and ourselves as your servants for Jesus' sake.

For God, who said, "Let light shine out of darkness," made his light shine in our hearts to give us the light of the knowledge of God's glory displayed in the face of Christ.

2 Corinthians 4:4-6

Being diagnosed with AIDS was the farthest thing from my mind, given all I was putting my family, friends, and church through. That, to this day, is the most painful aspect of my story. According to my beliefs and everything I had tried to embrace in my life, what I had done was shameful. I had put so much in jeopardy. My physical well-being meant nothing. The emotional pain of what I had done was so deep that dying would have been a welcomed relief from living with what I had done. My conflict was that I had always lived a life of grabbing life and kissing it in the face, trying to embrace joy and encouraging others to do the same. I had experienced some disappointments throughout my life, as we all do, and I had clumsily learned to cope and make the most of situations. I had been richly blessed and had lived a life that was so beyond anything I deserved. Life was too precious for me to give up at this point, and it was apparent that if I got through this at all, I could have a story to help others. One of the most significant banners that I had tried to hold high for others to see my whole life was the importance of learning from failures, pressing on, and making a useful application of lessons learned. Did I have the energy and the desire to do the same with my current situation?

I reflected on the times when my spirit had been contagious. I had to find a way to do the same with this situation. I was determined that the hurdle I was facing, as tall and as monumental as it was, would need to be treated no differently. My sin and HIV would not define me. To turn my back on making good of a bad situation would negate all that God had designed His plan of forgiveness of redemption to be.

CHAPTER SEVEN
Released to Go...Home?

With some convincing from my parents, doctors agreed not to send me to a nursing home. My parents knew that I would not be returning to my house. I, however, did not. I was placed into my parent's care, and it would be their home where I would go to recover. I remember the day I was released. I was dressed in clothes that no longer fit, and the journey from my room to the canopy at the hospital entrance was exhausting. I had not sat in an upright position for that length of time for many weeks. The outside air was refreshing, but it did not mean freedom. It meant going into another unknown world that left plenty of unanswered questions. The only positive thing that day was the smell of the tulips in full bloom outside the hospital. It was incredibly fragrant and in contrast to the stale smell of my hospital room.

I went home with my parents to my childhood home. I remember crying as I faced the reality of living with my parents as a forty-four-year-old man. I wanted to go home...my home. I wanted my bed, my things, and to be surrounded by the people that I was most familiar with. I had hoped that my homecoming circumstances would be quite different from what was unfolding. The hour-drive home was humbling. I was in yet another situation that was out of my control. I had no choice. I had no say, and rightfully so. I had sacrificed control of so many things with my indiscretion and missteps. Tears flowed as we pulled into the driveway as the reality of what was happening set in. My mom told me not to cry. She assured me that everything was going to be alright.

My parents assisted me as we climbed the stairs to the room that I had grown up in. This surprise and unexpected chapter in my life was not how my story was to end. This was not a chapter I wanted to include in my life's story. As they put me in bed, I stared at the four walls surrounding me. This home held memories of my youth. This room and house were the backdrops of my childhood. It was here where I had memories of fishing, playing with my dog, riding my dirt bike, playing with my Star Wars action figures, and doing all the things that children do. This home would now become a stage as my life with AIDS played out for, no doubt, an audience that was hiding in the wings waiting for the next act to start.

The bit of optimism I had gained during the final few days in the hospital began to wane as I felt increasingly sorry for myself. Thoughts of death, by my own hands, entered my mind. Satan planted seeds of doubt that I was nurturing. The doubt that I could get through this with any semblance of grace and credibility was growing. I allowed him to convince me that there was no reason to live. I was too much of a burden to my parents. They did not deserve this, and I played out various scenarios in my mind to bring my pathetic tragedy to an end. I was not in any condition or position to contribute anything positive to the lives of others. I no longer had anything left to give. I felt disposable.

I questioned everything that my life had been up to that point. I even began to resent the time and energy I had poured into ministering to members of the church. Why had I given so much? Why had I allowed my well to run dry? I found so many threads of injustice in my scenario.

My parents became my caregivers. I had lost everything. Confirming my suspicion, I was told that my home, car, and possessions were being sold. I can only imagine how exhausting and draining this experience must have been for those who were piecing together a plan financially to react to my sudden exit from work and income. My parents helped me secure my disability benefits which were made relatively easy to obtain given my impaired eyesight. We made the necessary arrangements to get the funds dispersed accordingly.

I had made mistakes. However, the results of my careless actions were not deliberate. They were, admittedly, selfish and thoughtless. Daily my illness reminded me of what I had done. It was hard to escape the shame, guilt, and embarrassment. It took a great deal of discipline to remind myself that God still loved me unconditionally. I remember finding the energy one day to mumble to myself the tune and the words of "Jesus Loves Me" in a desperate attempt to remind me of God's simple truth. There were days that I did well and days that I struggled horribly in remembering that I was still of value to God. Each day was a struggle to get on my feet emotionally. Satan was always trying to kick me back to the ground, and most days, I allowed him to do so.

There were too many pieces to pick up and put back together. Some pieces had removed themselves from the picture, which made the picture that was my life impossible to assemble. If you have ever tried to put a puzzle together and then realized that some of the pieces are lost, then you know how frustrating it can be as you long to see the completed picture. I would never see the image that was once my life again. If I had the energy and resources to come up with one, a new portrait would need to be created. I reminded myself that God had created the universe and that indeed, He could help me put my life back together in a way that would bring Him honor and glory. It would have to be by His hand if it were to happen.

CHAPTER EIGHT
A Portrait of God's Character

One afternoon, a turning point in my spiritual recovery was when my mother was bathing me. I was too weak to bathe myself. As I sat on the side of the tub, too weak to stand, my mother slowly knelt with a towel and began to dry my feet. She also put moisturizer on my feet and elbows as my skin had become dry during my hospital stay. As she carefully administered her loving care, God's Spirit took my thoughts to the story of Christ washing the disciple's feet in the Gospel of John.

When Jesus rose from the table to wash the feet of the disciples, He was doing the work of the lowliest of servants. The disciples were shocked and taken back at this act of humility playing out by the very Son of God. It did not make sense to them. Christ, their Lord and Master, was washing their feet. Their Lord and King was doing something that was typically done by the lowliest of servants. It should have been them washing His feet. When Jesus came to earth, He came, not as a king and conqueror, but as a servant to serve.

> "..."You know that the rulers of the Gentiles lord it over them, and their high officials exercise authority over them. Not so with you. Instead, whoever wants to become great among you must be your servant, and whoever wants to be first must be your slave - just as the Son of Man did not come to be served, but to serve, and to give his life as a ransom for many."
> Matthew 20:25-28

He came not to be served by others but to serve and give his life as a ransom. The humility expressed by His service with a towel and basin was painting a picture of what would become an act of sacrifice on the cross. His service was an act of love being given to all of us. He was intentional in His portrayal of being Lord of all and was disciplined and humble in demonstrating His desire to serve. He was not just interested in serving those in high positions. He was given as a gift to all, and His sacrifice would change the world forever.

If Jesus gave freely of His gift of forgiveness and salvation to all, why is it that we, as a church and society, often withhold forgiveness from some individuals? We prioritize sin, placing various sins on different levels and determining for ourselves what sin we will forgive and what sin we will not. How is it that we can sit in judgment when Christ, the very Son of God, died on our behalf, allowing each of us to receive His grace, mercy, love, forgiveness, salvation, and redemption? We negate all that God has put into His plan of salvation for our lives when we decide to sit in judgment. Judge is not the role we are given. Our part is to demonstrate Christ through our words and actions for others. Every person is a precious soul that has an opportunity to spend eternity with God in heaven. This opportunity for eternal life is not to be taken lightly. We must each play a part in sharing the message of God's sacrificial gift in and through His Son, Jesus Christ. There is no place for gossip, judgment, and pretending to know the details of what others may be painfully experiencing as they deal with the consequences of their sin. It can be reckless when we forget the fragility of life as people try to cope with the results of what they have done in relationship to their disobedience to God. That process is God's and not ours to manage. We, in obedience, need only to honor and follow His instruction. Christ's sacrifice covered all sin. His gift was for all people, and it is our privilege as His children to communicate that sacrifice and love to others. How else will others know His love, forgiveness, and mercy if not demonstrated effectively by those who choose to follow Him?

In that moment, when my mother was drying my feet and as I sat humiliated on the side of the tub, I realized that although I had preached about the Son of God for twenty-three years, I was seeing the very face of Christ through my mother as she cared for me with Christ-like love. At that moment, I was getting a first-hand picture of the real purpose behind God sending Christ to a lost world. I was lost. My self-worth was shattered. My on-going question was, "How could anyone possibly love me in this sinful and pathetic state?" Now, in full view, I see my mother loving me unconditionally. It was an example of Christ's unconditional love. I did not need to understand it. I did not need to know how it worked. I needed only to experience Christ's love and know that He was still willing to call me His child. He was willing to consider me as a part of His family. As His child, I needed to be embraced, not abandoned.

I am not able to tell you much about my former friends. Many disappeared. Some went as far as to hide from me by blocking me from accessing them through phone numbers and various social media outlets. Without words, they sent me a message. Many of these individuals were people I had helped through multiple trials in their own lives. They were close friends that I had loved and encouraged through the years. Many, too, had made their share of mistakes and had toyed with sin in their own lives. I wanted to be held accountable for what I had done, but the accountability for my recovery was two-fold.

Who would hold themselves accountable for the support and direction I needed? Most of my friends had moved on with their lives. I know now that the right kind of life is a life where one surrounds themselves with the right kind of friends. Some of my friends were far more than friends. I considered them to be family. Some were brothers that I never had and meant a great deal to me. They meant more to me than they will ever know. I know that I had let them down. There was something about me that they did not know. They will never know how much I wanted to tell them what I was going through. There were many times that I came close to opening up to one of them and seeking the help that I needed. How would they have reacted? Would they have been a source of support, or would their reaction have only added to the mess I had already made? Who could I have trusted with my secret? Unfortunately, I was finding that my fears and my hesitancy to share my problem with the church, to some degree, appeared to be justifiable.

I have now seen, first-hand, how people did, indeed, react. My experience has taught me that there are those within the church who are equipped spiritually and are willing to assist in carrying the weight of what life can bring and, sadly, many are not. Each of us must examine our hearts and prepare ourselves for this responsibility. The burdens are to be shared. That is what we are to do as brothers and sisters in Christ. We should never be caught unprepared to assist a hurting soul when the opportunity presents itself. This unpreparedness to help a hurting soul, perhaps, adds to the destruction of people more so than the sin itself.

CHAPTER NINE
God's Expectations for Love

It was God I should have trusted all along. It was God that eventually brought me through the storm and gave me the love and support I needed. He took my situation and beautifully weaved a safety net of support for me to rely on. He used people. Some of the people He used were not church people at all, but they knew how to love, accept and nurture me in a way that some, within the church, sadly, were not able to comprehend. I did not need criticism or reprimanding. I needed love. Scripture tells that without love, we are nothing.

If I speak in the tongues of men or of angels, but do not have love, I am only a resounding gong or a clanging cymbal.

If I have the gift of prophecy and can fathom all mysteries and all knowledge, and if I have a faith that can move mountains, but do not have love, I am nothing.

If I give all I possess to the poor and give over my body to hardship that I may boast, but do not have love, I gain nothing.

Love is patient, love is kind. It does not envy, it does not boast, it is not proud. It does not dishonor others, it is not self-seeking, it is not easily angered, it keeps no record of wrongs.

Love does not delight in evil but rejoices with the truth. It always protects, always trusts, always hopes, always perseveres.

Love never fails. But where there are prophecies, they will cease; where there are tongues, they will be stilled; where there is knowledge, it will pass away.

For we know in part and we prophesy in part, but when completeness comes, what is in part disappears. When I was a child,

I talked like a child, I thought like a child, I reasoned like a child.

When I became a man, I put the ways of childhood behind me. For now, we see only a reflection as in a mirror; then we shall see face to face. Now I know in part; then I shall know fully, even as I am fully known.

And now these three remain: faith, hope and love. But the greatest of these is love.

1 Corinthians 13:1-13

My situation was real. It was my life. It was not some kind of script, book, or movie that the church had an option of writing themselves out of when the chapters got too tricky or unpredictable. That is not how God's Word describes Christianity. We are to be a body with all parts working together.

Some refused even to let me ask for their forgiveness. How did they justify that mentality? I realize that forgiveness can take time and that it is not an easy process in cases such as mine, where I had built a situation of mistrust. I am not pretending that my sin was not difficult for people to understand. However, it was not something for them to understand. I did not even understand it myself. I simply needed their love. I needed their support. Understanding my sin and getting the help I needed was between God, the friends I could trust, my counselor, and me. Being still and knowing that God was in control would have probably served all of us well as we made decisions based on our human nature and our want to control the circumstances we were facing. Trusting God and being still enough to listen should have been our priority.

> *Trust in the Lord with all your heart and lean not on your own understanding; in all your ways submit to him, and he will make your paths straight.*
> *Proverbs 3:5,6*

It is up to each of us to partner with Christ, trust in Him, and make things right with Him. The rest we must give to God and trust Him to lead the way.

Child of God would now become the new defining label that I would try to wear (HIV and all). I was given the honor of wearing that label from birth, but self-doubt and the torment I experienced did not allow me to believe it fully. I had lived a life longing for people to know Christ and the peace that He brings. I was sincere in my ministry, passionately so, but at times it came from something I was looking for and had yet to find for myself. Unfortunately, it was elusive for me, given my misguided approach in trying to find it. It was a joy that I was trying to find in people and my relationships when, in fact, it really could not be found there at all.

I tried to give others what I wanted for myself, but in the meantime, I was repressing my private grief. I lived a life of making others feel at ease and preaching a message of joy that I so very much wanted to experience myself. It was a facade that I was hiding behind. The expectation I had created of what others could expect from me was impossible for me to maintain.

Being a minister made it more difficult because people, typically, will not let a minister be human. We expect our minister to be a superhero of sorts, never having a bad day, able to come to our rescue regardless of what might be going on in the minister's life, and always expecting a smile and an enthusiastic charm coupled with an animated personality. I could not possibly let people in on the secret that I was lonely and insecure. That was not acceptable. There were times when I did convey that I was tired or stressed to someone, and it was usually met with a churchy "this too shall pass" or a quick diversion to talk about something going on in their own life.

Even a few family members enjoyed having a monopoly on the stress and martyr factor when serving the church. If I dropped the veil to show the humanity behind my minister title, it was met with an awkward inability for people to understand. I found that it was not worth the energy involved in explaining to people that I, too, was human. I could never articulate it without coming across as needy or wanting attention.

Many of my conversations, even with strangers, were centered on them, and most of these conversations I enjoyed. After all, listening and talking people through life's problems was why I entered the ministry in the first place. The reality that I was not prepared for was that very seldom would people pause long enough in their conversation with me to ask me about my family or well-being. It was usually all about them. In ministry, this is all par for the course. We need to do better in teaching people to listen. It will only be through our ability to listen effectively that we will discern the need in a person's life and speak or act accordingly.

My diagnosis with HIV had proven me right about what I had suspected about some people. It was all about them. Most people, in my experience, only seemed interested in how my diagnosis and sin had impacted them or how it made them feel. They responded accordingly, never giving much thought to the sin, the sinner, and their role in the healing. It was a disturbing glance into the heart of people. What I needed was to see the nature of God's forgiveness and care. What I got, from some, was characteristically human and disappointing. We, as a church, I included, need to be better than that for one another. We must!

To be clear, I was not the only person hurting and suffering the consequences of my sin. Many were caught innocently in the crossfire of what I had done. Some had to step away from me and focus on managing the difficult circumstances. My situation was multifaceted and with many levels of hurt and mistrust. My appeal and outline of what I understand the church's role to be in a case such as mine does not merely apply to the sinner. Often, as in my case, others are affected by the sin that was committed and need intentional assistance and guidance in their healing.

I had read, believed, and taught about God's forgiveness and mercy. Still, given my situation, I was now able to see Him and His character through the people who were unconditionally providing my care and healing. Thankfully, there were those in my life that were prayerfully making the best application of what they understood God's provisions for love and forgiveness to be. They helped me understand that HIV would not define who I was. The virus was secondary. I was still Danny. HIV was a part of who I was, but it was not who I was, nor was the sin that brought the virus into my life. I was still the child that God had created me to be. I had made my mistakes and paid the consequences for what I had done, but I was still a child of God. I was reminded that situations like mine are the very reason that Jesus was given to us as Redeemer and King. God does not expect us to grovel in our sin. He provides us with a way out, which is the beauty of who He is. Jesus was given to us as a gift of salvation to experience a joy, not based on people and circumstances, but rather a joy rooted firmly in Christ. For it is Christ who is constant, loyal, and eternal regardless of what might be going on within our lives.

Shame and guilt are not characteristics of God, and if I were to be a picture for others to see of my Heavenly Father, I knew that I had to put those feelings aside. If I chose to portray those characteristics in my life, I would negate the power of God's plan for redemption. It was not going to be easy to convince myself and others of God's forgiveness and cleansing blood, but my only option would be to be an example of God's light and His voice of encouragement.

CHAPTER TEN
HIV Treatment Begins

With time, the meningitis was brought under control, and doctors were ready to begin my HIV treatment. With my "off the charts" HIV viral load and a damaged immune system, the possibility of fully recovering was minimal. Doctors would experiment with finding the right combination of medications to bring down the HIV viral count. I looked at my doctor appointments as buying time until AIDS eventually placed the final nail in my coffin.

I recall the morning that I had my first appointment with my infectious disease doctor in Columbus. I was still weak, and up to this point, the focus had been on treating the meningitis. I had not given much thought to my HIV status. The idea of having HIV was too overwhelming. With everything else I was dealing with, I managed to ignore it. I could not ignore it now. It was time to take steps toward treating HIV. My parents borrowed a wheelchair from a friend as I was still too weak to walk independently. With the wheelchair loaded in the trunk and me in the back seat, still barely able to hold my head up, we started the hour-long trip. What would the doctor say about my AIDS diagnosis? Was this a terminal situation, and would I be given a timeline when I could expect the infection to take my life? I had no idea what this diagnosis meant for me. I was uninformed and uneducated on HIV.

When we arrived, my mother pushed me in the wheelchair to the clinic while my dad parked the car. As we proceeded down the long hallways of the infectious disease facility, I could feel my heart rate getting faster and my emotions getting more and more out of control. Sitting in an AIDS clinic could not possibly be my life. Entering the small waiting room, I was surrounded by men who looked disturbingly sick. Did I look as ill as they did? Were we all here for the same reason?

What stories could they tell? Were they getting the care and support they needed, or were they facing AIDS alone? How long had they had it? How did they get it, and were they getting better? I was one of them. I had joined their club. I was a part of a community that I had only read about in magazines or heard about in a story on the nightly news.

As I sat in the waiting room, waiting my turn for my appointment, my innate desire to put everyone at ease was kicking in, but I was too weak to manage a focus on anyone but myself. I was afraid to make eye contact with another patient. What would I say? Why did I think I needed to say anything at all? I guess the minister in me could not help my tendency to want to talk to them and hear their story and offer a word of encouragement. I had something in common with these men. I knew, to some degree, what each of them was going through, and I wanted to help, but I knew I could not. I had myself to consider.

I was called back for my appointment. I was assisted as I stepped onto a scale. I was still nearly fifty pounds under my ideal weight. I was taken to a room to wait for the doctor. It was a cold room adorned with HIV and AIDS posters. I resisted reading the information. I was in denial that I was there at all. The doctor came in with a robust smile and cheerful demeanor. She assured me that everything was going to be alright, and she communicated to me that it was her job to find the right combination of drugs to control my HIV. In my mind, I could only imagine that this was what she told everyone in my situation. It was her job to give people hope. I was trying to discern if she was buying me time and keeping me comfortable or thought that I would be alright and live a normal life. After all, this was not what I knew about AIDS. I was under the impression that it was terminal. I expected a life that would be lived out with stigmas, doctor appointments, blood transfusions, and hospital stays. I convinced myself that her positive attitude was a mask to hide her concern and keep me optimistic. She discussed HIV and told me how it affects the body and why my diagnosis was full-blown AIDS. I did not know that there was a difference between them until that point. HIV is a virus. AIDS is the destruction of the immune system and your body playing host to an opportunistic disease due to a depleted immune system (mine was fungal meningitis) and a significant viral load of the HIV virus. I had all three.

A combination of drugs was decided upon, and a prescription to pick up at the hospital pharmacy was written. All of which had significant side effects. With the prescription of drugs came the question of how I would come up with the money to get the prescription filled. The combination of medications prescribed would cost me thousands of dollars for a ninety-day supply. Even with insurance in place, the thought of managing the cost of the drugs was beyond overwhelming. I was assigned a caseworker, and an assistance program was put into place. Having a caseworker was a humbling experience. The paperwork that I had to file to get assistance was exhausting in every way imaginable. I managed to find a way to get my first round of HIV treatment and prayed that the combination of drugs chosen for me would help me get better, but I had my doubts.

I returned to the doctor in 4 weeks. After going through the motions of taking the first round of HIV drugs with little expectation of getting better, doctors reported that the medications were working amazingly well based on my first round of blood work. Miraculously, within four weeks of being on HIV medications, my viral load dropped significantly, and my immune system began to recover to a small degree. My immune system was on the rebound and enthusiastically so. The report from my doctor was good news.

As my immune system began to rebuild itself rapidly, the process took a toll on my body. My body was reacting with headaches and nausea. My first thought, not knowing it was the immune system at work causing me to feel sick, was that the meningitis had returned. I did not want my mom and dad to know that I was not feeling well. They had been through so much, and I wanted to protect them from the stress and exhaustion of another hospital stay. I tried hard to pretend that I was feeling alright, but with time my body showed too many outward signs that something was not right. After hiding my symptoms for fear of landing back in the hospital, I finally confessed to my parents that I was sick and probably should make a trip back to the emergency room regardless of what that might mean.

CHAPTER ELEVEN
Second Hospital Stay

My fear became a reality. A second two-week stay in the hospital was necessary to suppress my immune system. The immune system's recovery had to be slowed down in that it was causing swelling throughout my body. It was unexplainably out of control. The doctors successfully managed my immune system's recovery as it climbed back into the normal range. While recovery of the immune system is not unheard of, it is quite rare especially given how mine managed to rebound so quickly.

Unfortunately, the good news was short-lived. With this hospital stay, my bloodwork showed signs that something was not right within my body. It was something that the doctors were not associating with HIV or meningitis. My bloodwork was indicating the possible presence of cancer somewhere in my body. Had cancer, too, taken advantage of my depleted immune system? Time would tell. With the news that my bloodwork indicated a serious problem somewhere within my body and knowing that I was far too weak to fight any additional illness, I gave up. I pleaded with God to let me die. Another battle was too much for me. I figured that we would all be much better off if I were dead in my limited and shallow mind. The talk of biopsies, scopes, and additional spinal taps was more than I could handle. I was terrified, and the misplaced feeling of being alone in my battle took over my emotions. I had nothing and no one to live for. I wanted nothing more than for all the drama of my circumstances to come to an end.

Still far from where I had been before my diagnosis, my cognitive skills had improved, which now put me more in tune with my situation. Understanding the critical nature of my situation made my second hospital stay more difficult as I could piece together the severity of my circumstances. My heart hurt. There was not a distraction big enough to keep me from thinking of all I had lost over the past couple of months. My mind was full of thoughts that I could not piece together.

Easter was fast approaching. I could only observe the signs of Easter from my window at the hospital. The trees were showing signs of buds, the hospital flowerbeds were full of flowers, and it appeared that people had put away their winter coats in exchange for lighter jackets. The long winter days gave way to warmer temperatures and brighter, longer days. Unfortunately for me, it was a reminder that I would not be spending time outdoors, mowing a yard, enjoying my cherished tomato garden, or sitting on my patio watching my hens pick at an abundant supply of dandelions. With so many things to think about, most of which I did not understand, my mind became a breeding ground for doubt and depression.

It was my second stay in the hospital that I hit rock bottom emotionally. Again, with my cognitive skills coming back, I was more able to see the impact of what I had done and see the consequences' reality. My thoughts of the new reality for my life were heavy and sat on my heart like a boulder that was impossible to move. I asked my nurse if it would be possible for me to have a hospital chaplain visit me. Other than my parents, up to this point during my second hospital stay, no one had come to visit me. I was now seeing, first-hand, how much all those hospital visits I had made as a minister must have meant to people. At times, I had been so critical of people during my ministry when they complained about how no one from the church had visited them. I was now on the other side of that scenario and knew now how meaningful a minister's visit could be. Hospital stays can be a lonely experience, not to mention all that I was dealing with emotionally and spiritually.

A hospital chaplain came to my room to talk to me. Talked he did. He talked about how busy he was and how there was not enough time in his week to get everything done that he needed to do for Easter Sunday that, by the way, was fast approaching. He spoke of how he could not wait for Easter to be over and then quickly added that Easter being over would mean knowing that a crazy summer of church camps and mission trips would be upon him. He complained about his church and their selfish appeals for his attention. He never paused once to ask about me or why I had asked to meet with him. It was excruciatingly painful to listen to him. My heart was breaking, and he was too into himself and his one-sided conversation about himself that he did not see the reality of my situation. It was a reminder of what I had suspected about people, but in a moment of weakness and desperation, I thought I would find an exception. I had done nothing more than set myself up for disappointment in requesting for him to come and visit me in the first place. I grew angry. I needed an ear to listen. I needed prayer to be offered on my behalf. I needed to hear the words of God's encouragement. I found myself just wanting him to leave. I thanked him for his time and apologized for requesting to see him, given the busy week he had described to me in detail. I remember thinking to myself, "Is that what we, as a church, look like to the world? Have I ever sounded like that? Have I been a part of that picture for the past twenty-three years, and if so, is it any wonder people are not interested in joining us for worship?" I was now on the other side and getting a picture of what sinners, like me, need from the church. I needed love and acceptance, and I was having a hard time finding either one, and it broke my heart for the church and me.

Perhaps it was then that the thought of one day communicating what I saw in the churches' response to my illness and sin entered my mind. It was not about me. The picture was much bigger than my situation. The appropriate response to a situation like mine was either elusive for some or being ignored. Was the glimpse of a problem I saw a symptom of a larger problem within the church? Love and acceptance, two core teachings of Christ, were lost in a sea of people going to church and not seeing the importance of being the church that God needed and wanted them to be.

Again, I must emphasize that my concern was for the church and me. I had been a pastor for twenty-three years, leading, teaching, and developing programs to train my flock to minister effectively. From the perspective that I was now viewing the church from, I concluded that there was something, perhaps universally so, that we were not understanding about God's expectation for ministry and meeting the needs of a lost and dying world.

A flyer had been delivered to my room with an invite to attend an Easter church service to take place in the hospital's surgery waiting room. The surgery waiting area was a part of the hospital that I had spent countless hours in with my church members as they waited on news of their loved one's surgeries. The church service was something I wanted to attend. On Easter Sunday, I asked permission from my doctor to attend. I insisted that I make the trip to the service on my own, and even though it was several floors down from my room, the challenge of walking to the service was something I looked forward to tackling. I made my way to the service in my hospital gown, robe, and textured socks. Exhausted from the walk, I tried hard to focus on the message of the worship service. I tried to be thankful that I could physically attend the service. Attending the service would mean walking on my own down the hallway to the elevator and then making my way to the church service on another floor of the hospital. Making the journey to the service was a big deal.

I remember feeling a sense of independence that day. I was trying to take steps forward emotionally and spiritually, but I could only think of the congregation I should have been leading that day. Were they thinking of me as much as I was thinking of them? Did they feel the void that I was feeling, or had they already filled their void with something or someone else? Did they even feel a void at all, or had I only meant something to them when they needed something? I felt disposable. I felt like a piece of trash tossed to the curb.

As I sat by myself in the very hospital lobby where I had sat with so many church families in their time of need, I thought to myself, "Where are they now that I need someone?" I had been there for them during surgeries, babies being born, cancer treatments, car accidents, heart by-passes, and biopsies. I had been there, in that very hospital lobby, to comfort them when their loved ones had breathed their last breath. I had prayed with families in so many corners of that hospital, now I was sitting alone. Where were they?

Easter Sunday was a profound time of reflection. It was a day that I remember being grateful and focused, but it was also a day when I felt about as alone as I had ever felt in my life.

I remember eating lunch in my room, wondering what was going through the minds and hearts of those I missed. Did they know I was getting better? Did they care? What were they thinking? I was seeking answers to the mysteries and behaviors of the human heart. I was also trying to determine what God's expectations were for my heart, given my situation.

What did my response to my circumstances need to be? Of course, my heart needed repaired. It was broken. My concern for figuring out others and their attitudes toward me, my indiscretion, and illness, needed to be replaced with figuring out my own heart if I were to recover. My heart finally centered on thinking about myself and my recovery and leaving others' hearts and minds to be a matter between them and God. I had two options…to live or die. If I chose life, I wanted it to be a life of joy and not a life of existing with the stigma of

AIDS and shame. Did I have the faith and emotional energy to press on and face my demons? I also knew that many were cheering me onto a finish line of failure. I had to choose to prove them wrong by embracing the promise of redemption and putting my best foot forward in what I knew would be a long journey.

I ate my Easter dinner alone that day in my hospital bed. I remember eating a salad and a sandwich, and I recall reminiscing on the various meals I had eaten on Easter in the past. The hams, mashed potatoes, and mom's pickled eggs (yes, pickled eggs) that I had enjoyed for so many years on Easter Sunday sounded so good. I reflected on the innocence of my youth and the fond memories I had of searching for Easter eggs with my siblings at my grandparent's home. As I reflected, I remember wishing for a do-over with my life. I wanted so much to take away the pain I had caused for those I loved and wondered that day if they would ever be able to find their joy again.

Yes, at times, I had blamed others for my destructive behavior. That mentality only added to the emotions of what I was experiencing. I had to put my blaming of others aside and deal with the reality of my situation and know that I could not change the past or the hearts and minds of others. If I were to make progress, I could only be concerned about the piece of the mess that I could fix and take responsibility for mending. I wanted to change everything, and I grew frustrated as the realization of knowing that I could not change a thing finally settled into my mind. This was now my life. I single-handedly created a problematic situation for others to deal with as they, too, were caught in the consequences of my sin. I grew more depressed that day, and, again, I convinced myself that death would be a welcomed relief.

The ups and downs of my emotions were starting to take a toll on me. One minute I was optimistic, and within moments I could be frozen by depression. As that scenario played out over and over daily, it became increasingly painful and exhausting. The closest thing I can compare it to is having a chair pulled out from underneath you over and over. Each time it is pulled out from under you, you feel a little more foolish and a little more humiliated until you decide not to even bother with sitting in the chair at all, but simply lying on the floor in a state of asking yourself the question of, "Why bother?"

Later that Easter Sunday afternoon, as I sat alone and depressed in my hospital room, I heard a familiar voice enter my room. It was my older sister, Debbie, and her boyfriend, Rod. They had not completely forgiven me. They had not told me that, but I could determine that for myself. They certainly did not pretend to understand how I had allowed myself to be drawn into the sin that had led me into the consequences I was experiencing. I had disappointed them along with so many others in my life. That said, none of that seemed to matter to them that day. Those things did not matter in that they were there to see me on behalf of Christ, and it was evident that they were trusting Christ to work them through the issues they had with me in time. They were exercising spiritual discipline. They knew that they needed to be there for me but could not do that themselves, given their hurt, mistrust, and the disappointment that they had in me.

It was apparent that they were not visiting me by their strength. Debbie and Rod relied on God's Spirit to lead the way. They made their visit, their words, and their actions all about me as they had come to make themselves available as a tool in the hand of God to minister to me. They had set their thoughts and feelings about me and my situation aside. I could tell that day that it was not easy for them to be there. I sensed both, especially my sister, was still struggling with me and what I had done. They made themselves available to God so that they could, if possible, offer me a word of encouragement and a glimmer of hope. They will never know how much their visit meant to me. Again, Debbie and Rod, another example of people being willing to be the very face of God for someone in need.

CHAPTER TWELVE
Our Call to Ministry

Surrendering ourselves to God's will and allowing ourselves to play a role of support and encouragement in the life of one in need is not easy. Take my situation for example. It was multi-faceted with many angles to consider. Where does one begin in providing ministry in that type of situation? Ministry might mean having to play a role of support for someone others have written off as unworthy or for someone you are not enthusiastically keen on helping. While taking on the self-appointed role as judge, some see offering help to one who has done the unthinkable as negating or softening the consequences that one must pay. The severity of consequences need not be our concern. Healing and restoration should be at the heart of assisting those in need. Many do not take steps toward offering support given the lack of confidence in themselves to provide the level of support they feel is needed. This interest in not wanting to misstep is commendable and understandable, but we must be more prepared as tools to be used in God's hand.

Each of what I have described treads on underestimating what an amazing God can and wants to do through ordinary people. The Bible is filled with fascinating stories of ordinary people doing extraordinary things while partnered with God and staying in line with His purpose. We must open ourselves to allowing Him to provide the attitude and skill set needed to accomplish His purpose. We make it far too complicated. I know, for me, it was the small things that meant the most as people offered their assistance to me. It was holding a hand, telling a story to distract me from the thoughts of my situation or merely the presence of one who cared enough to sit by my bedside saying nothing at all but, in their presence, provided a measure of reassurance that I was not alone.

Supporting one another and allowing God to work through us is vital if we are to maintain the balance of all that is needed to pursue God's will for ourselves and in providing ministry to those dealing with a crisis. We deal with circumstances that can drain us of what is needed to function as productive and emotionally healthy human beings. If we are not careful, we find ourselves unable to provide what is necessary to spiritually maintain the energy to help others. Our lives become inundated with the daily grind of the schedules we create. Some are over-committed to programs and activities within the church, not leaving time for themselves to work on self-spiritual preservation or leaving windows for time dedicated to personal, one-on-one ministry with those in need.

We do not always have the appropriate coping mechanisms to take on life and the difficult circumstances that can come with it. When our world is full of stress, all of us need the support that God has made available. God has promised us the tools to achieve what seems to be an impossible task to accomplish. When wanting to tackle a chore around the house, have you ever experienced the frustration of knowing that you do not have the proper tool needed to complete the job? If a job is to be accomplished we borrow or invest in the equipment or tools required to do the job and do the job well. We make it a priority. In ministry, we need to do the same. We need urgency to complete the job and the willingness to invest in making sure that we are equipped with the proper tools. Having the appropriate tool when the need for ministry presents itself is a blessing, and being prepared, contributes to the joy that we receive in our ability to make a difference in the life of another.

Even with the little obstacles in life, God wants us to experience joy. This joy is found in our opportunity to rejoice in a celebrated victory. We celebrate many things in life. We plan celebrations for birthdays, anniversaries, retirements, graduations, and holidays. When we conquer a difficult situation in life, should we not pause and recognize the victory and the people who may have played a part in us achieving a victory? That achievement, in and through God, is what He longs for us to enjoy as He creates a path for us to experience His joy. The joy may not come directly from His hand but can very often come through the hand of support of someone He has purposed to offer their assistance to us. The balance we must find is to be willing to humble ourselves to receive help from others graciously and provide support to others in a manner that reflects the attitude that Christ demonstrated so beautifully throughout His ministry and service to us.

I had always found God to be a source of strength and encouragement, but what I also needed in my time of darkness was the love and support of others. Given what I was facing, I needed them in numerous ways. I needed to feel their hand holding mine physically. I needed words that were cheering me onto a spiritual recovery. I wanted, more than anything, to get better. I did not pretend that I had not hurt people or did not have a problem. I wanted to accept responsibility, but I was overwhelmed and needed help knowing where to start and how to do what was expected. My thoughts were not of why I needed to take responsibility but rather of how I needed to take responsibility. I had so many pieces to take responsibility for that I did not know where to start. I needed assistance in assembling a starting point.

The thoughts and feelings that I was experiencing were complicated to figure out all alone. I needed people. This is by God's design. As His children, we are referred to throughout scripture as a family, a flock, a body, and an assembly. These indicate a connection and need for one another to function as individuals and as a unit. God has made us with unique gifts. Serving with others can open doors to discovering the joys of the fellowship experienced while serving together and can reveal the strength found in different gifts coming together for the good of a common cause.

For the sake of God's plan and design, the church is called upon to stand together as one. This is not to say that we, as tools in God's hand, can only stand with those who are without sin. Jesus stands with sinners. This does not commend sinful behavior but rather inspires acceptance of the people who have sinned. In Him, standing side by side with sinners, He demonstrated His expectation for the partnership needed to bring spiritual healing to those in need. His willingness to spend time with sinners involved sacrifice not only for the time and resources involved but also in the sacrifice that was made in what others thought of Him in doing so. He was criticized and questioned, but He stood firm in His resolve to offer support to those who needed it. He was an example of one who wanted to help others carry the weight of their sin, the stress and social disconnect that came with it. It is an example that we are to follow, but He, too, was subject to the balance that must be found between ministry to others and maintaining one's spiritual well-being.

Those who serve within the church will tell you that they are no exception from dealing with the difficulties and stresses of life. For some, given their responsibility and desire to assist others, it is greater than anyone can imagine. I do not share this to create a pity party for myself or those serving in full-time ministry. I share this as a reminder that ministry can be demanding. Without careful attention to one's own spiritual and physical well-being, it can deplete you totally of what is needed to preserve one's spiritual and emotional health. Those in full-time ministry need to be encouraged to maintain spiritual well-being just as they encourage others to do the same. If a shepherd is going to step into the role of being an example for his flock, then the shepherd must be fit mentally and spiritually to invest the time and energy required to set that example. For many years, I dealt with the expectations placed upon me. Again, expectations that I was aware of before taking the sacred vow of going into full-time Christian service.

Not many of you should become teachers, my fellow believers because you know that we who teach will be judged more strictly.
James 3:1

Unfortunately, in my youth and naïve enthusiasm to serve, I failed to consider the human factor and understand the required discipline it would take to provide for myself the on-going maintenance needed to serve while not allowing my spiritual well to run dry.

Those serving the church in a full-time capacity are as human as the people they serve. Unfortunately, some have been conditioned through their unique ministry experiences to implement the art of creating a façade over their emotions as they strive to survive in a world of service to others that can be exhausting. This practice is not healthy. At times and to a fault, they are careful not to let anyone get a glimpse of what might be a weakness in their ability to maintain the balance between life and ministry. While ministers try to be energized and prepared to assist those in need, ministers have bad days just like anyone else. Yes, they have voluntarily placed themselves into the fishbowl of ministry. Before ever stepping up to the sacred desk of service, they should have realized that the church and God would hold them to a higher standard of accountability (and rightfully so).

When we see a minister fall into sin or a difficult circumstance where they cannot uphold the banner of encouragement and service for others, do we not owe them the same support and love that we are asked to afford to everyone? Does their sin bring with it an immediate consequence of isolation? As one who has walked this path personally, I think not. The fact remains that they, too, are human and are covered by the blood and sacrifice of Jesus Christ. I am not suggesting that this is a pass to find oneself free of the consequences of sin, nor does it free anyone from being held accountable for their actions. Scripture is clear that those who choose to lead others spiritually and put themselves into a leadership position are to be held to a greater level of accountability. This level of accountability is biblical. However, they need to be treated with the same level of love and concern in their moments of weakness. They have the same need to be encouraged to take strides toward their recovery and a renewed spiritual state of well-being. When it comes to making poor decisions or stepping into a sinful action, no one is immune. We are all human.

The lures of temptation and sin are everywhere. Life can be challenging and, even those in full-time ministry can become worn down and spiritually complacent. If they are not careful, they can find themselves caught off guard spiritually.

> *Be alert and of sober mind. Your enemy the devil prowls around like*
> *a roaring lion looking for someone to devour.*
> 1 Peter 5:8

Some see their minister as an all-powerful, spiritual human and have the expectations that their minister, outfitted in a mighty armor of biblical proportions and spiritual cape, is capable of successfully maneuvering through life's struggles and coming to the rescue of those in need. That is the image that many within leadership would love to display. Still, realistically, those in service to others and those relying on their help must understand that people have limitations whether they are a minister or not.

I made a poor and careless decision. I participated in a sinful action. In doing so, I jeopardized so much. I put myself in a situation where people could justifiably state that I was not the man they thought I was. When the veil of my sin was lifted, there was something about me that people did not know. A part of me became foreign to those who thought they knew me. The image that I had tried to uphold withered and, in an instant, I became the one in need of support.

CHAPTER THIRTEEN
Assisting the Weary

God's Word illustrates for us, within the pages of the Old Testament, an account of when a leader showed that he needed the support of those around him. No, his weakness was not related to a sinful action, but the story beautifully illustrates the need for all of us to engage in unwavering support of one another. While he was willing to do what was expected of him, this man of God was tired. His spirit was unquestionably generous, but his flesh grew weary with every passing moment of service to those He was trying to encourage. He needed the dedicated support of those around him if he would succeed and maintain the work that God had purposed for him to do.

> *The Amalekites came and attacked the Israelites at Rephidim. Moses said to Joshua, "Choose some of our men and go out to fight the Amalekites. Tomorrow I will stand on top of the hill with the staff of God in my hands."*
>
> *So, Joshua fought the Amalekites as Moses had ordered, and Moses, Aaron and Hur went to the top of the hill. As long as Moses held up his hands, the Israelites were winning, but whenever he lowered his hands, the Amalekites were winning.*
>
> *When Moses' hands grew tired, they took a stone and put it under him and he sat on it. Aaron and Hur held his hands up - one on one side, one on the other - so that his hands remained steady till sunset.*
>
> *Exodus 17:8-12*

Moses offered his support to the Israel army by announcing that he would stand at the top of a hill as Israel battled against the Amalekites. He planned to hold up high the staff of God so that the Israel army might see this as a sign of his encouragement as they pressed on in their goal to win the battle. Moses wanted the staff to serve as a sign of his support for them as an army and as a sign of God's almighty presence. But as Moses held the staff of God, he grew weary. Unable to hold the staff for the army to view, the Amalekites began to win the battle. Aaron and Hur, who had accompanied Moses to the top of the hill, realized what was happening and acted by taking a stone and placing it under Moses so that he could have a seat and rest. Together, they proceeded to assist Moses in holding up the staff of God so that the Israel army might continue to be encouraged and, in turn, prevail as victors over the Amalekite army. God's purpose was fulfilled, but it took teamwork. One man was not called to do it alone.

Many need support. The needs of people are diverse. Some situations can be difficult and will take a team of support, but for most, it takes merely the heart of one willing individual. In the story of the children of Israel going up against the Amalekite army, it took a team of people to keep the group focused and on track. The support offered led to a victory, bringing glory to God and serving as a testament to the power of serving and supporting one another.

We spend time talking about ministering to those outside of the church, but we must also find a balance supporting one another within the church. I have seen situations unfold where the church was critical and judgmental of someone within their community. In attitudes that are not characteristic of God, we waste valuable time coming to the aid of hearts that are hurting and of those who can benefit from an appropriately placed application of God's love and forgiveness. There must be an immediate desire to help, and that desire should be coupled with a spiritual preparedness. If there is a desire to help, discipline is critical in putting a long-lasting, practical plan for ministry into place. Taking the time to put these components into place will establish a foundation that will not just change a life for a short time but forever. Seeing this type of ministry play out in the life of one in need is incredibly satisfying and brings a joy only found when we are in line with God. In seeking God's direction for ministry, you can successfully hit the target as to what is at the heart of the ministry at hand.

God's desire for us to experience joy is seen in His commitment to supporting us in our support of one another. Like any good father, God enjoys observing His children being there for one another in good times and bad. God knows the importance and benefit of a community of people combining their skills to achieve a goal far more significant than themselves. My observation of some within the church is that there seems to be contentment with passing along criticism and making no plan for healing and guidance when it comes to those that have lost their spiritual footing. It is often not from a lack of wanting to help but rather from a lack of knowing what to say or do. In the awkwardness of not knowing what to say or do, we resort to doing nothing. Therefore, I emphasize the importance of being prepared. Preparedness for ministry is a vital part of the task that we are commissioned to fulfill by God. Just as police officers or firefighters take vows to be prepared to do their jobs at a moments' notice, we must, too, be ready to do our job as a church when it comes to jumping into action and assisting those in need. We cannot afford to be caught off guard or surprised when it comes to an opportunity that presents itself. Time is essential, and our response must be immediate, intentional, and thoughtful. We must carefully choose every step in bringing people to Christ and introducing them to the never-ending source of unconditional love and hope.

Assisting in the process of building someone back up to their intended design is no easy task. However, this is something that we, as children of God, must be prepared and willing to do. We, as a church, get so busy and diluted with programs and ministries that we forget about the importance of one-on-one personal ministry. We must be intentional in this. The heart of what we are called to do as a church is to love and to convey a sincere acceptance and love toward people, one soul at a time. If that were not the case, Christ would not have emphasized it as much as He did throughout His ministry. He met the sinner where they were, and His focus became their situation and their unique, hurting heart and wounded soul. His approach to personal ministry is one we must embrace.

As a boy, I remember playing for hours with blocks. I would design and build towers and buildings as tall as I could stand and sometimes use a chair to build my tower even taller. It took time as I balanced the multi-colored blocks and selected, oh so carefully, what blocks would serve best regarding strength, height, and stability. Eventually, my joy would come from not building my tower but rather tearing it down. As crazy as that seems, my pleasure would come when, with one swift kick to the base, the tower I had worked on for hours to build would tumble to the floor. The fall was accompanied by laughter and screams of letting the whole house know that I had destroyed something. It gave me power and a sense of control. It was mine to build and mine to destroy. Well, this is not the case when it comes to people. People are designed by God. They are His creation. It is God who has put the time and energy into creating them into what He wants them to become. He has put the various blocks of their lives into place.

For God did not appoint us to suffer wrath but to receive salvation through our Lord Jesus Christ. He died for us so that, whether we are awake or asleep, we may live together with him.

Therefore encourage one another and build each other up, just as in fact you are doing.
1 Thessalonians 5:9-11

It is not up to us to be a part of the demolition crew when a child of God finds that they are at risk of falling. In that moment, we put on our spiritual tool belts to assist with the building process as we recognize the need for support.

Moses was dealing with a difficult situation. The church is no exception to having to deal with difficult people and problems. We must look deep within ourselves and to God for answers. When we do not, our human nature can quickly take over. When it comes to matters of encouragement and the restoration of a sinner in trouble, God's Spirit, within us, is always the best avenue to provide the ministry that is needed.

If we look to others solely for answers, it has been my experience that we will be disappointed. It all goes back to that human factor. People will let us down. Therefore, I must emphasize the value of trusting God and allowing Him to work in and through our lives. We do that by stepping out of the way and providing space for Him to work. Much of what we try to bring to the ministry table can be way off target in that we are human and limited in what we can see of the big picture. Forfeiting what we believe the big picture to be takes faith. Very often the big picture is not for us to see. When we allow ourselves to be used by God, we become the avenue by which His hope can be delivered. When we discipline ourselves to be a vessel for Him to provide what is needed, we are assured that the message and actions are on target to serve His purpose not only for that moment but also for eternity.

I remember watching television on the afternoon of January 13, 1982. I was a freshman in high school. I had come home from school, grabbed a snack, and sat down to watch some TV. My program was interrupted by a special report. The special report was broadcasting live from the crash site where a passenger plane had crashed in Washington,

DC, plunging into the Potomac River. Air Florida, Flight 90, while leaving the Washington National Airport (now Ronald Reagan Washington National Airport), had lost altitude, slammed into the 14th Street Bridge, and plunged into the frozen river while trying to take off in a snowstorm. Striking the bridge and having settled into the icy river, 74 people on board perished, as well as four motorists on the bridge.

I watched as a handful of survivors surfaced in the icy waters of the Potomac. They were desperately clinging to debris and trying to stay afloat. Still, the freezing temperatures, jet fuel, and frigid waters made it impossible for them to function physically or have the mental wherewithal to help themselves. A helicopter dropped life rings into the river, trying to place the rings as close as possible to those fighting for their lives. Some of the rings were just inches from those visibly within moments of drowning, but in their distress, they did not have the strength or vision to reach for the life-saving device. As I watched the situation unfold, I noticed many people on the shore trying to help.

At one point, a woman found her way to a life ring and was being carefully lifted to shore, but in her weakness and disorientation, she slipped out of the ring and back into the water. She began to fade beneath the surface of the frigid water. At that moment, I remember coming up out of my chair and saying out loud, "Somebody, help her!" Of course, that statement came easy for me, not experiencing the horrific conditions of what was the reality of being there. Within seconds of me saying that the camera caught something that I will never forget. A man on shore removed his coat and dove into the icy water to assist the woman in need. There was no question he had put his own life in danger given the situation's cruel and inclement conditions. In my mind, I thought that I would now see two people drown on live TV. The few seconds it took for him to reach the woman seemed like an eternity. His heroic act is forever in my mind. He assisted her as the two of them clung to the life ring and were pulled to safety.

The man sensed an urgency to help. He put his welfare and interests aside to sacrificially help someone in need. He knew that the woman would have drifted below the water without his help and been lost. I will not pretend to know the thoughts that must have gone through that man's mind in those final moments before he chose to enter the water and save that woman. Still, undoubtedly, it was a feeling of thinking he had something within him that could make a difference, and he chose to act on his instinct. He not only changed a life, but he also saved a life, and, in doing so, he made an impact on me, a fourteen-year-old teenager.

Our faith must come into play when deciding to help others and allow others to help us. Choosing to trust God to help us be a voice of hope will allow us to serve people. Putting into place an all-important layer of humility will give us the ability to enable others to help us. The ministry that flows from the hand of our all-knowing God when He partners with a humble and willing servant is a vibrant and beautiful display of useful service that can change a life for eternity.

My inability to recognize this truth was what led to my fall. I wanted something within myself to pull me out of the trap that I was in when, in fact, the solution to my problem fell somewhere among friends and other resources that my pride kept me from utilizing. The answers to life's most difficult circumstances are found in Christ working through His faithful servants in our lives. We must trust others and give people reason to trust us, and, most importantly, we must trust God to work in all situations. The Lord has created each of us with abilities that can contribute to the ministry of the church. God longs to orchestrate ministry within the church by using His children. We must be more disciplined in listening to God and in seeking His direction for what our part will be in His plan to bring His love and salvation to a lost and hurting world.

Every individual and church experiences various chapters of discouragement and disappointment. It can be disheartening, and it can set a church back considerably from moving forward with all the things that are important in the life of a church. The distraction of a church or individual not prepared for a crisis is a victory for the adversary. It is in those times of seeing a need (big or small) when we must, together, assist one another in holding up the staff of God as Aaron and Hur did for Moses. We have a tendency, as a church, to make that process more complicated than it needs to be. We overthink what God's expectations are for us when perhaps our role in the support of someone can come in the form of a kind word, a card, a phone call, a text, an email, or a small act of kindness.

If we desire to have a healthy and effective ministry in bringing people into a saving relationship with Jesus Christ, we must generate a contagious and willing spirit of support towards one another. If the world does not see us supporting one another, why would anyone want to be a part of a family of believers or go to church? As I found myself on the outside looking in, this question haunted me in knowing that I had been a part of that picture. It was a picture that broke my heart because, as I pondered this issue, I found myself reflecting on many situations where people fell through the cracks as those that could have helped stood by watching and playing judge from a gallery of apathy and ignorance.

Are you an active part in holding up a banner of support for others to see, or are you instrumental in knocking it out of the hands of those who are? Do your words and actions build others up, or do they destroy? Are you a participant in moving the message of God's plan of salvation forward, or do you give reason to those who observe your life to question the church's purpose and the role that we each must play within it?

> *Instead, speaking the truth in love, we will grow to become in every respect the mature body of him who is the head, that is, Christ.*
>
> *From him the whole body, joined and held together by every supporting ligament, grows and builds itself up in love as each part does its work.*
> *Ephesians 4:15,16*

When I was in high school, my family took a trip to South Carolina. My parents permitted me to take a friend with me. We stayed in a cabin overlooking a lake. One afternoon, my friend and I decided to rent a boat and row it out to a small island in the middle of the lake. We sat side by side, and each of us had an oar. It was hard work rowing that boat, and we had to make sure to row evenly and equitably to assure that we stayed on target in reaching the island. We reached the island, spent some time exploring, and decided to make our way back to the cabin. As we rowed back to shore, a storm was approaching. We doubled our efforts in rowing back to shore before the storm hit. We wanted nothing more than to be safe on shore and back at the cabin. In our frantic effort to row, one of the oars got away from us and drifted out of reach. With one oar and now, with only one of us rowing, the boat went in circles. We could not make good progress in that we could not work together, and we no longer could take advantage of the tools needed to row the boat successfully. Eventually, we did manage to get safely back to shore, but it was not easy. We were operating outside of the design of the tools we had been given. Therefore, the task at hand was much harder than it should have been.

Two questions must be asked. Are all of us doing our share of rowing when it comes to the local church's ministry and, are we using the tools we have been given?

CHAPTER FOURTEEN
Enough Faith to Expect and Anticipate

In the book of Acts, we are given a great example of one who offered support and encouragement and who had a positive attitude toward everything and everyone. His name was Barnabas, and he has become an excellent reflection of encouragement. Encouragement was so much a part of his life and the core of his ministry that his friends stopped calling him by his given name of Joseph and began calling him Barnabas, which means "Son of Encouragement." His very name described the center of who he was as a man and as a follower of Christ.

Encouragers have the measure of faith needed to place their trust whole-heartedly in God's hands, and they know that God can change a situation so that it works out for the good of all those involved. They see the best in every situation and every person. To summarize, they believe that God can and will do what is best for His children. The encourager also has the ability, and patience, to not meddle in God's ability to manage a situation. They live their lives uplifting others with words of encouragement and assuring those around them that God will find a way through any problem that some may find impossible to overcome. Their cup is always half full, and their prevailing attitude is that good things are not only possible, but that good things are to be expected and should be greatly anticipated.

Encouragers are seekers. They seek out good things not only for life in general, but they seek out what is good in others. When dealing with someone who lacks self-confidence and faith in God, they highlight what is good in that person, helping them see their unique character and abilities that they can contribute to others' well-being. Viewing people and situations through God's eyes, encouragers always see the potential for reconciliation with Christ and with one another, allowing us to be created new in Christ.

Therefore, if anyone is in Christ, the new creation has come: The old has gone, the new is here!

All this is from God, who reconciled us to himself through Christ and gave us the ministry of reconciliation: that God was reconciling the world to himself in Christ, not counting people's sins against them. And he has committed to us the message of reconciliation.
2 Corinthians 5:17-19

For me, I was holding tight to the church and praying that they would hold tight to me, love me, and direct me in the direction that I needed to go. My heart needed restoring. The old needed to pass away, and I needed someone to convince me that I could anticipate a redeemed heart and life, and I needed help to develop a spiritual roadmap to get there. I needed an encourager to help center my faith in God and to then help me see, with their optimistic eyes, the signs that God was, indeed, paving a way for me to get back on my feet spiritually. Through Christ, the church, and the encouragement they had to offer was my only hope. I recognized it as my one trustworthy source of recovery if I were to recover at all. The question remained, would there be people in place and willing to help me embrace the light of mercy and forgiveness that I needed? It was not going to be something that I had the strength to do myself. I would need encouragement to be strong and steady in my recovery. We must understand the depth of what we are called to do for one another and for those who are lost and hurting. It is a matter of maintaining someone's soul and assisting them in getting back on track spiritually. Recovering spiritually is an eternal matter and is not to be taken lightly.

The church, serving as a retreat for a spiritually lost world, is where the introduction of redemption is often made to those searching for it. I can't stress enough how important a sense of urgency is in taking Christ to others. As I took steps to manage the mess that was now my life, I needed Christ and those willing to rally my soul to seek, find and call upon God's redemption. I knew that I could not do it alone. My life and circumstances were too hard and overwhelming. I needed the support of those within the church, and many were striving to get it right. It would be those individuals that I would need to place my hand in as they guided me to a path of redemption.

I am intense about the purpose of the church and each member's purpose doing their part within it. I have been on the other side of ministry. I am a sinner and have experienced the hardship of being spiritually void. The urgency is real. There is far too much at stake. It is a matter of life and death. Depending on our ability to get this right, it could mean eternal life or death for the one who is lost. It is a matter of heaven or hell. I did not understand that fully until I was face to face with my mortality. I was standing at death's gate as a sinner. This is no exaggeration. I was at risk of easily passing from this world into the next and never having the opportunity to adjust my sail and finding the peace that I longed for. My question was haunting, "What would become of me should I pass from this world amid my ruined state and not having reconciled myself with Christ?" What would be my eternal fate if I did not get a chance to ask for forgiveness for the sin that had me so entangled in a web that I found impossible to escape? Would death take with me the sin, the secrets, and shame that I had yet to turn over to Christ? A sense of urgency is vital. Loving and accepting people and affording them Christ and the redemptive power that He offers is important. We have no way of knowing the spiritual condition of someone's heart and the need for the remedy of Christ's plan of salvation that they may have.

Our mission is to love, accept, and lead people toward the forgiveness that God offers through the redemptive plan and person of His Son, Jesus Christ. We are called to do nothing less. This is our purpose within God's design for our lives. God depends on us to convey His healing path to those around us. There may be lives within our midst who are silently dealing with things that we cannot possibly imagine. Perhaps there is a "Danny" in your life that needs a safe door to walk through. We must make sure that we offer them a safe hand to hold and a trusted ear that is willing to listen. Keeping something so life-changing and precious to ourselves is robbing those in need of knowing God. The peace that a loving relationship with Him is a peace that so many in our world are needing. God has given His best for us. Why should we give anything less than our best when it comes to taking Him and His message of hope and joy to a world that desperately needs it?

Therefore encourage one another and build each other up, just as in fact you are doing.

Now we ask you, brothers and sisters, to acknowledge those who work hard among you, who care for you in the Lord and who admonish you.

Hold them in the highest regard in love because of their work. Live in peace with each other.

And we urge you, brothers and sisters, warn those who are idle and disruptive, encourage the disheartened, help the weak, be patient with everyone.

1 Thessalonians 5:11-14

Encouragement and lifting one another up in Christ comes not from our own opinions and sometimes careless understandings, but by what truth God's Spirit is speaking to us. I know that opinions were immediately formed regarding me and my situation. Some views of my situation were accurate. Most opinions were created based on speculation, bits, and pieces of the truth, and remnants of what some had added to my own, and very personal, story. Some added their thoughts to my story so that it could make sense to them. The truth is that it didn't need to make sense to them. It didn't even make sense to me, and I was the one at the heart of the conflict. Our role in encouraging people is not to understand anything other than that we are to love and extend care while constructing a plan to assemble the pieces of their lives back together. Adding to an already tragic story is nothing short of irresponsible and makes a complicated situation worse. Yet, many of us find ourselves doing that very thing by offering an attentive ear to some who revel in the joy of gossip. The shoes that people walk in are unique. Their backgrounds and reasons for doing things are often deeply rooted in their past experiences and their fears of an uncertain future.

As we prepare ourselves spiritually to serve others effectively, we must remember that we, too, are sinners. Failing to personalize Christ's sacrifice and applying it to our own need for redemption and restoration is a mistake. It is a path that can lead to a misplaced, spiritual arrogance. Remembering that Christ's sacrifice was made for all gives us an advantage in ministry in knowing that each of us have flaws that Christ has already sacrificed Himself for. This gives us something in common with those we are striving to serve and those we are serving alongside. This commonality puts everyone as equals at the foot of the cross. This same reflection also reminds us of our dependency on Christ for the joy and peace we seek.

The hope that we seek is afforded to us at a price, and it is a price that we are not asked to pay. The human elements of what Christ paid in the giving of Himself must be remembered and understood. Christ was a life, a man, and a savior given unselfishly for each of us by God, our Heavenly Father. He had friends and family. His mother watched in horror as they crucified Him on a cross. His body was human in every way. He bled and felt pain. He was spit upon and beaten as He felt the torment and the wide range of emotions felt in every moment of His last hours. As Christ, the sacrificial Lamb was offered for each of us; a bright light was being prepared. That light would shine upon each of our paths, leading the way for us to walk in the light and affording us the advantage to steer clear of the darkness that can so easily cause us to stumble and fall. Without Christ removing the darkness of sin in our lives through His sacrifice, our lives would continue to be a path of missteps on the trail of darkness that Satan has paved. Failure to offer our support to others in our on-going spiritual warfare will give Satan the upper hand.

Given my experience, I was humbled by the reality of knowing that I, at times, was not what I should have been for the people within my life and ministry. I am sure all of us have had our shining moments in helping others, but I fear that we play "church" or go through the motions of what we think Christ wants and needs us to be. We need to be more intentional when it comes to allowing the ministry of Jesus Christ to play out within our lives. The process is beautiful, and what a blessing it is for those who get it right and who have the joy of being a tool in the hand of God as He works through them in affording someone redemption and forgiveness.

So, put on your armor and prepare yourself for battle. Stand confidently on the hill of everything good and pure so that those in need of encouragement can see the staff of God held firmly in your hand. Hold it high! Give those in need of strength something to press towards and look forward to! Be willing to be used by God, and if you grow weary in holding up God's message of hope and salvation, my prayer is that there will be someone standing next to you who is willing and prepared to assist you in your desire to serve Him! Press forward in doing what you know God has called you to do. An impactful ministry will play out in your life and will be a picture of Christ for others to see.

CHAPTER FIFTEEN
A Name Placed on My Heart

While still in the hospital for my second stay, I experienced something, unlike anything I had ever experienced before. The experience has me scratching my head to this day and has left me with no other option but to leave the questions attached to it in God's hands. It is difficult to explain and is something that I have hesitated to talk about up until now. A name was placed on my heart while in the hospital. It was a name that I was familiar with, but to my knowledge, it was the name of a woman that I had never met. We had attended the same high school. She was a few years younger than me, and I don't recall that our paths had crossed at any point. I knew that she had married a ministry friend of mine, and they had ministered as husband and wife at a small church not far from where I had served as a youth minister right out of college. Unfortunately, I also knew that they had divorced a few years into their marriage. I knew little about this woman that was placed on my heart.

Her name, "Melissa," would come to me in the middle of the night in dreams. The dreams, so intense and confusing, would wake me up and occur several times throughout the night and day as much of my time, while hospitalized, was spent sleeping. I would wake up disoriented with the haunting question of wondering what this name could mean, if anything. With all I had to think about, why was this woman being put on my heart? It was disturbing. It was nightmarish for me. I made myself sick, trying to suppress the thoughts of her name. There were more important things I needed to think about. The thoughts and dreams of this woman named Melissa were playing with my emotions. I would wake up shouting her name. My nurses would ask me about Melissa. I, embarrassingly so, would have to admit that I did not know why I was shouting her name out in my sleep.

With everything else that was filling my heart and mind, why was this random name tormenting me? I managed to put the name "Melissa" out of my mind with time. Little did I know that I would only be able to put the name "Melissa" out of my mind for a short period of time. This "Melissa" was waiting in the wings to be yet another face of God for me to see.

My second hospital stay, at long last, was successful in getting my blood work and spinal fluid levels to where the doctors were comfortable in allowing me to be released back into the care of my parents. The concern that I had cancer was put to rest with a painful bone marrow biopsy. While still struggling emotionally, doctors decided that I was physically strong enough to go home...again.

CHAPTER SIXTEEN
Home, Again, and Determined

After nearly two weeks in the hospital, my immune system began to stabilize, and I was released, once again, to go back to my parent's home. I remember stopping for lunch on the way home. This was a real treat in that I had been eating hospital food for two weeks and eating at a restaurant was an opportunity to do something normal for the first time since my diagnosis. My parents thought it would do me good to get some fresh air and experience a change of scenery.

My enthusiasm turned to terror as I was reminded, by the situation, that physically I was still frail, and my eyesight was still unable to make out the details of my surroundings. As I walked from the car, with assistance, to the restaurant entrance, I felt as if all eyes were on me and that everyone knew. I was convinced that my illness was evident to those observing my slow journey to the door. It was reminiscent of how I felt during my first stay in the hospital when I took my first walk. It was as if I was wearing a sign. My mind crippled me more than anything. Satan was still at work and wanted nothing more than for me to feel trapped in his grip. My enthusiasm turned into weeping, and I wanted to go back to the car. Pressing on and once inside the restaurant, I recall needing to use the restroom and having to be accompanied by my dad. I felt like a child and, in my limited vision as to how my life would look moving forward, thought this would be my life from this point on. I remember ordering a sandwich that I had ordered so many times before, only to discover that I no longer had the strength or appetite to eat it. I felt frail and helpless. Every aspect of my being was suppressed. Who was I? What, if anything, could I possibly do to change the course of the physical, emotional, and spiritual dive I was taking? The scary thing was that I knew I could not change my path. It had taken a detour from what was normal and from everything I had taken for granted throughout my life. I was being forced into a position where God was the only source that could save me from my present circumstances.

I was in a state of brokenness, and my only hope was the possibility that God was preparing, within me, something that could make good of a bad situation. I see that now but, at that time, I was convinced that I was down and out for the rest of my life. I could not imagine being used by God, being a productive member of society, or looking at my situation as an opportunity to encourage and help others. It was just too much to imagine. If God still had a plan for me, it would take time before I was able to believe it and to be able to do my part in making it happen.

Being dismissed from the hospital and arriving at my parent's home again was as emotional as the first (if not more). I was a mess emotionally, but my body, while still feeble, began to gain strength. Walking from my bedroom to the bathroom was a big deal. I remember making that fifteen-step trip without help and feeling a great sense of accomplishment. However, I was not to make the trip down the hallway without my parent's help because in my weakness, my legs, without warning, would completely give out. My mom placed a bell next to my bed to ring when I needed to get up. I couldn't do anything without their help. I felt like such a burden. Their days were centered around me and my needs in that they had become my sole caregivers. Their lives were not their own. I could see the love in their eyes, but I could also see disappointment and frustration. Physically, they both looked worn and exhausted. It was apparent that my illness was taking a toll on my parents. I wanted to gain strength and become more independent. My body seemed to grow stronger with each day.

Being home, somewhat mobile, and able to have visitors, I had an issue with clothes. I was about fifty pounds lighter than what I was before my hospitalization. My mom collected clothes from thrift stores and garage sales. She would bring home clothes in sizes that I had not been able to wear since being in middle school, and, with me only fitting into clothes made for young boys, I had to adjust to looking ridiculous. Each morning, I would piece together clothes the best that I could while trying to maintain some sense of dignity. Of course, nothing compared to the horror of mom grabbing old clothes out of my dad's closet for me to wear.

My limited choice of clothes was not as much the issue as having to admit that I needed help getting dressed. Unable to find the necessary strength and flexibility, my mom would help me get dressed each morning. I cannot begin to describe the experience of being in your mid-forties and your mom having to put on your socks and shoes as you hang your feet childishly over the side of a bed. Putting on anything that had to be placed over my head was more than I could manage. I was too weak. My morning routine was something that I looked forward to. I did not have much reason to get dressed, but it gave me something to do. Getting dressed gave me a small glimpse of what was once my life. Of course, my morning routine was now in deep contrast to what, just a few months earlier, was getting ready and walking out the door looking like a seasoned professional. I missed the days of getting dressed and looking forward to a day of meetings and tackling a list of things to do. Any task that I could incorporate into my schedule gave me a sense of purpose.

My only option for any form of exercise meant taking walks back and forth in the upstairs hallway. Those short walks eventually led to me being able to walk up and down the steps as I tried to gain strength and rebuild my muscles. I remember gaining confidence and somewhat mastering a stride reflective of what I remembered walking to be. Much like a toddler learning to walk, I gathered mom and dad in the family room to show off my new skills. As days turned to weeks, my renewed coordination and strength enable me to take longer walks.

With the warmer temperatures, I would take short walks outside accompanied, at first, and then eventually, permitted to go by myself if I promised not to go too far from the house. A few of my parent's neighbors were kind enough to walk with me giving mom and dad some much-needed time to themselves. Those walks, the fresh air, and having normal conversations about things other than being sick, inspired me and slowly gave me the hope that I was, indeed, going to get better.

My eyes sight, while improving, was still lacking. I had difficulty reading, identifying faces, and my depth perception was not improving. One of the more difficult things I dealt with visually was that I could not see a contrast between things that were the same color. Meals were a struggle in that I could not differentiate a helping of mashed potatoes from a serving of cottage cheese. It did not matter. I was told to clean my plate no matter what was sitting in front of me. My mom made me eat everything on my plate, ensuring I was getting a healthy and balanced meal. She was doing everything within her strength to ensure that my health would continue to improve. I was also dealing with memory issues. Trying to recall memories and various people from my past was difficult for me, which was frustrating. Perhaps, in some divine way, that was God's way of keeping me from the hurt that may have come along with the memories I was trying to recall. I remember looking through my cell phone and seeing names and numbers that meant nothing to me. There were names that I could not put a face to. This was upsetting to me because I knew I had only entered the names and numbers of people closest to me, like family members and people within the church. I reviewed some of the names and numbers with my mom. She helped me recall some of the names and connect the role they had played in my life.

I was still weak. I could not look at myself in the mirror without crying. I had become skin on bone. I had no muscles to speak of, and it was a task to sit at the table for a meal without excruciating pain. My back was not strong enough to keep me in an upright position for very long. Standing was much more comfortable and doable than sitting. As determined as I was to find redemption and heal spiritually, I was also determined to recover physically. I would not allow AIDS and my sin to define who I was. I was still a child of God, and I had a life to live for Him, and with every ounce of my being, I was not going to let this knock me off my feet and distract me from God's purpose in my life.

For those who are led by the Spirit of God are the children of God.

The Spirit you received does not make you slaves, so that you live in fear again; rather, the Spirit you received brought about your adoption to sonship.

And by him we cry, "Abba, Father." The Spirit himself testifies with our spirit that we are God's children.

Now if we are children, then we are heirs - heirs of God and co-heirs with Christ, if indeed we share in his sufferings in order that we may also share in his glory.

Romans 8:14-17

I had a reason to live and tell my story and the tale of the lessons I had learned. God opened my eyes to truths that I had never seen before, and those truths were not going to be revealed to me in vain. I wanted to share what God was doing in my life emotionally, spiritually, and physically.

Many logistics needed to be taken care of regarding me pressing on and accepting my new life. I did the best I could. That was all I could do. My parents tried to take care of me, but it was evident that they were not going to guard me from my sin's consequences. They knew that there were hard lessons that I needed to learn. My finances, my medication, phone calls that needed to be made, and taking responsibility for what I had done were all my responsibility. They were putting a roof over my head, feeding me, and assisting in my recovery, but my parents were not protecting me from the realization of what I had done. There was no sweeping my sin under the carpet. I wanted it all to go away, but my heart told me that the circumstances would never truly go away. I needed to learn how to manage the hurt and the consequences of what I had done. The price I was paying was unbearable and unquestionably life-changing and challenging for those I had hurt, for they, too, were affected by the devastation I had caused. The new life I was finding was not the life I wanted, but I was thankful that I had any life at all. I tried to discover and imagine what my new "norm" would be.

On my birthday, my mother brought the family together to celebrate. I could not help but question what we were celebrating. Mine was now a tarnished life and, in my mind, was not to be celebrated at all. I did not deserve to be celebrated. I was filled with anxiety given the fact that a celebration was being held in my honor. I appreciated my mom's plans for the family to gather for my birthday, but it only added to the pain of knowing that my party was not complete. There were empty chairs at the table that should have been filled by the ones I treasured the most. My family was in pieces, and the most important pieces were not present. The party was an endless charade of everyone going through the motions of what we all thought a birthday celebration should be. It was emotionally draining. Even the messages within the birthday cards, given to me that evening, were questioned in my mind. With each birthday greeting I read, I thought to myself that there was no way anyone could have possibly read the card before handing it to me. If they did, they could not have possibly believed the message conveyed within. The greeting card industry does not make birthday cards that read, "Happy Birthday to our son who has humiliated the entire family" or "To my loving brother who messed up his life." This would be my new life, or so I thought. I assumed I would spend the rest of my life wondering if anyone could love me as a person and especially as a person living with HIV.

Walks to the end of the street soon turned into me learning how to ride a bike again at forty-five. Learning to ride a bike as an adult is a humbling experience. Sit-ups and push-ups were done in the privacy of my bedroom. My efforts were all but laughable. I would use anything that I could get my hands on as I tried to find ways to get my body back to normal. It was not easy, but I did not want to look sick. I wanted to look healthy. I wanted to have a strong physical body to accompany the emotional and spiritual progress. I wanted to feel and look complete. While my spiritual mending took priority, my physical well-being and appearance were something that I knew I needed to work on if I were to ever get out from under my parents' care.

Mentally, there was a great deal of work to do as well. My memory and ability to piece together thoughts were difficult. I don't know if that was from my mind being so overwhelmed or if the lingering effects of the meningitis were preventing me from processing thoughts and ideas. I lost pockets of time from my memory. Many names and places that I should have easily recognized were beyond my ability to recollect. There are many people from my past that I cannot remember or recall the part that they played in my life.

One day, while out on a walk alone, I told myself that I would try to run. I had conquered walking, but would my legs and brain work together in harmony enough to allow me the coordination and the physical strength that I needed to run? I was willing to give it a try. I remember looking around, making sure that no one was around to witness what might be me falling flat on my face. While thinking that I might be able to run, I imagined my first attempt to do so would look as awkward as a toddler making their first attempt to walk. It was clear. I was confident that I was out of view. A row of pine trees conveniently hid me from my parent's home, and I was out of sight.

I accelerated my walk to a very slow and, might I add, awkward, jog, lifting my knees and taking the strides needed to increase my speed. It hurt physically to get my feet off the pavement, and, to my surprise, placing them back on the pavement in a way to keep me steady and evenly balanced was just as painful. With every stride, it was like lifting my feet out of wet concrete. It reminded me of a reoccurring dream that I have of being chased but suddenly lose my ability to run and, if I can run at all, everything is in slow-motion. With each step, my feet became a little lighter. My confidence grew as my speed and gate increased to what I would describe as a very silly-looking and unconventional run. I was running…by no means fast, but I was painfully and joyfully running. As far as I was concerned, I was Secretariat, and I was headed for the finish line at the Belmont Stakes to claim the Triple Crown. As I turned the corner and headed towards my parent's driveway, my imagination filled my head with dramatic theme music as if this moment was a made-for-television movie that was playing out for the world to see. It was a life-changing moment. It was a moment that I will remember for the rest of my life.

I refer to that moment today to gain inspiration and motivation. Running, something I had done my whole life and, quite honestly, was very good at, back in the day, was now something that I realized was a gift. It was a gift that I had taken for granted. It was an ability that I had lost. God had given me what I needed to rediscover the simple pleasure and joy of putting one foot in front of the other and making strides towards a desired destination. The gift of mobility was something that God, once again, was returning to me as a blessing. Not only had I taken huge strides physically that day, but that moment helped me in my pursuit of continuing to take giant steps forward spiritually as well.

I planted a small garden that spring, knowing that I had to do something to stay active and keep me physically and emotionally engaged with something other than the heartbreak I was going through. I had to get permission from my doctor to be around dirt as my meningitis was fungal. With my immune system still climbing into the normal range, my doctor gave me the green light to garden. I enjoyed the process of cultivating, planting, and caring for something other than myself. It was not much, but it was mine. I was learning that God could still use me to impact something positively. I was a broken tool, but a tool God was using despite my brokenness. I eventually learned that my hard work and determination could bear fruit in the garden, but I had a bigger question for God. I would stand and look at my garden from my bedroom window and wonder if I would ever again bear fruit spiritually in the life of another. I believed that I could. I thought I was being prepared, perhaps, for something more significant than I could imagine. If that were to happen, I knew that my heart would need to be cultivated, seeds would need to be planted, and my soul would need to be nurtured. Could I do it? The answer was no. Could God do it? The answer was a resounding YES!

I have learned in life that acting on our own seldom produces spiritual fruit. My experience has taught me that any success of eternal value requires God's help and a willingness to surrender to His Son, Jesus Christ. It is only in our connection and relationship with Him that we can bear spiritual fruit of any kind.

Remain in me, as I also remain in you. No branch can bear fruit by itself; it must remain in the vine.

Neither can you bear fruit unless you remain in me. "I am the vine; you are the branches.

If you remain in me and I in you, you will bear much fruit; apart from me you can do nothing.

If you do not remain in me, you are like a branch that is thrown away and withers; such branches are picked up, thrown into the fire and burned.

If you remain in me and my words remain in you, ask whatever you wish, and it will be done for you.

This is to my Father's glory, that you bear much fruit, showing yourselves to be my disciples.

John 15:4-8

CHAPTER SEVENTEEN
The Confession

With time, I became strong enough to go to church with my parents. My immune system had grown to a point where my doctor had permitted me to be around people. I would be attending my home church. It was the church that I had attended as a child and teenager. Not only was it the church I attended growing up, but it was also the church I had served for nearly ten years following my graduation from Johnson University. I had served the Wilmington Church of Christ in Wilmington, Ohio, as their Minister to Youth. The thought of returning to church (any church) was scary. How would I be received? I was still thin and feeble, and the stares that I felt were not imagined as I walked into the sanctuary with my parents to find a seat. I was convinced that everyone knew every detail of why I was there.

Upon finding our seats, a well-intended woman welcomed me and told me how thin I looked, and asked me about my ministry and family. I do not think she was aware of my situation. I sheepishly smiled and told her it was good to be back in Wilmington while ignoring her question. I felt horrible for my parents. I had embarrassed them. I had become that blot on a perfectly good piece of paper that I had warned other people about becoming. I was the blemish, and I was confident that the dark spot on my life and ministry was all anyone saw of me and my forty-five-year-old life. Did they know what I had done? I knew I had been placed on the church prayer list months earlier during my hospitalization, but did they know about the virus I was living with? Again, those were all questions that I could not answer and were concerns that were out of my hands to control. I searched for something I could control and for something I could do to take steps forward to spiritually hold Satan at bay. I had always lived a very public life up to this point, given my ministry, music, and active involvement within the communities I served. Experience told me that people like to talk and, if they do not have details, they will make a story up. I had already set enough fires without Satan adding fuel through people and their apparent need to add to what was already a tragic story of sin and consequences.

That morning, throughout the worship service, God's Spirit was calling me to make a public apology to my home church and to those I had served. Not only did I know I needed to confess my sin publicly, but I needed to use this opportunity to be an example for others to follow. What did I have to lose? I needed to admit my sin, and I needed to ask for forgiveness. Beyond that, other than taking steps forward from there, there was not a whole lot I could do as far as helping others deal with the mess and heartbreak I had created. I had displayed how one can get into a tangled web of sin. Could I possibly lead the way in setting an example of how one finds a way out? A healthy dose of God's truth needed applied to the circumstances, but could I do it? Did I have enough credibility to demonstrate that even my situation was not something that had been shattered beyond God's repair?

My understanding of God's Word is that confession is the first step one needs to find God, His peace, and a path to recovery.

If we claim to be without sin, we deceive ourselves and the truth is not in us.

If we confess our sins, he is faithful and just and will forgive us our sins and purify us from all unrighteousness.

If we claim we have not sinned, we make him out to be a liar and his word is not in us.

1 John 1:8-10

As the end of the service came closer and closer, I imagined what I might say should I go forward and ask for a moment to speak. Who was I to think that I had anything worth saying? What would be the reaction of the congregation to see me go forward? Would the minister feel obligated to hand me the microphone? Would he let me speak at all? Answers to these questions did not come, but I knew that I needed to go forward regardless of the outcome. If I could manage enough nerve to take steps toward the platform, I felt sure that God would lead me in my words. I wanted my heart to be sincere, and I wanted to seek forgiveness from a congregation that had meant so much to me throughout the years. They had taught me in Sunday School, helped me with my Vacation Bible School crafts, led me in youth group, encouraged me through college, and received me onto their staff as Minister to Youth. We had made a significant investment in one another through the years. I needed to seek their forgiveness.

An awkward silence fell over the congregation as I stepped forward. Being short in stature, I felt it necessary to step up onto the platform. With the microphone in hand and trembling, I began to speak. I wept. I stumbled over my words while asking for forgiveness. I nervously stated that I had put so much in jeopardy by a decision I had made. I asked for forgiveness, explaining that their love and acceptance was what I needed the most as I planned for my recovery. I don't remember much about that moment. I do remember experiencing a sense of peace in that I was doing what God has told each of us to do within scripture. I was confessing my sin and asking for forgiveness. I knew that this was a step in the right direction. I felt, too, that in my flawed and human state, I was somehow shining a small light for others who might be struggling with a secret sin. It was Christ who shined that day. It was just one of those moments that only Christ could have orchestrated. His light was shining through a dark cloud and was seemingly preparing us to find our part in what would need to be my path to redemption. What role each of us would play was yet to be determined, but God would be faithful to orchestrate that as the pieces of my spiritual and emotional healing came together.

> *So, Christ himself gave the apostles, the prophets, the evangelists, the pastors, and teachers, to equip his people for works of service, so that the body of Christ may be built up until we all reach unity in the faith and in the knowledge of the Son of God and become mature, attaining to the whole measure of the fullness of Christ.*
>
> *Ephesians 4:11-13*

This scripture emphasizes the importance of each person within the church, working together by offering support to one another and being committed to reaching the lost with a message of love. That is what I needed from my church. I needed to be loved, and I needed a place to belong and that, for the most part, is what I received in the days and months to come as the Wilmington Church of Christ became a place of retreat and rest while I took steps toward recovery.

My confession had sparked a great deal of thought and emotions among the Wilmington congregation. With Dale, their senior minister, at the helm, the congregation joined me in my journey. Many shared with me that they had been moved to take steps forward in confronting their struggles that day. Some were moved that day to confess, with time, the various sins that they, too, had kept secret. God's Spirit moved that day. I had some members of the congregation tell me later that my confession and interest in seeking help had encouraged them to seek counseling for issues they had dealt with for many years. It was a good day on so many levels. We, as a body, were making a practical application of scripture. We were seeing the benefits of applying God's truth, and many were brought together that morning as God's Spirit moved a congregation to help a brother in need. I could not have taken my steps forward without them.

I discovered that morning that even in my flawed state, I could still shine the light of Christ for others to see simply by following His Word and obeying His instructions for my life. His desire for me that morning was for me to publicly confess and take responsibility for what I had done. In me doing my part, He responded with a fantastic wave of encouragement and mercy from a congregation that rallied enthusiastically to bring me back into the flock.

Following the service and my confession, numerous people made their way to greet me with hugs, tears, and encouragement. Amid all the people who greeted me that morning, one woman did not introduce herself to me at all. I did not recognize her. She hugged me. Her embrace was different. The only way I can describe the hug is to say that if I could imagine being hugged by an angel, that was it. It was warm, sincere, reassuring, and coupled with one of the most beautiful smiles I had ever seen. The woman stepped back from me, began to speak, and then embraced me once more. Unable to speak due to her emotions, she stepped back, looked me square in the eyes, and then departed. As the next person stepped forward to hug me, I lost her in the crowd. This woman, her hug, and her countenance were special. There was something unique about her, and she had been a blessing by her very presence. She connected with me without the use of words. Who was she? Why was I so taken with her smile, hug, and Christ-like Spirit that shined bright in her eyes that day? It played out in my mind as her being a caped superhero who swooped in at that moment, hugged me, and left me to wonder, "Who was that woman?"

CHAPTER EIGHTEEN
The Church and My Path to Recovery

Christ has embraced each of us and has reassured us that we are loved. He has let us know that we have His support and that He will be a strong pillar that we can lean upon in our times of need. In encouraging Christ's love and acceptance, I do not mean that the church aimlessly love and accept people who are in over their heads in sin, nor do I mean to insinuate that words of correction and discipline are not pieces of the healing to be implemented. I am also not trying to paint a picture of the sinner and the church where accountability and direction are not a part of the equation. It will be in love and in our desire to embrace scripture, discipline, guidance, accountability, and correction that God will move a congregation to love and nurture a sinner back to spiritual health. All of which I have mentioned are a significant part of what the church is called to do for those who have lost their way. I was fortunate to be in the care of such a loving and nurturing congregation. Dale, the Senior Pastor, and the leadership of the Wilmington Church of Christ, took their responsibility to me and my recovery seriously.

The support offered to me had conditions attached to it. I was connected to a Christian counselor, a spiritual mentor, a small group Bible study, and numerous individuals who weekly asked me tough questions and who expected honest answers. I was given reading materials coupled with reading assignments and questions that were to be completed and discussed in my weekly appointments with Dale. I was given direction concerning my prayer life. Yes, at times, I grew frustrated and beaten down. Still, each condition, assignment, word of accountability, and piece of stern and spiritual advice, was offered with an unquestionable portion of love. Dale would frustrate me at times by speaking the truth. The truth often demanded having difficult conversations and being forced to deal with the painful emotions and actions that I had tucked far away within my heart and mind. There were times he made me mad with his never-ending challenges to face my fears and to take the necessary steps to put them behind me forever. Dale was just what I needed. I grew to trust Dale, and he had endeared himself to me as someone who cared deeply for me as a member of the flock. He was disciplined enough to hold me accountable and focused enough not to make it about him or the church. His encouragement was firm, yet gentle. Most importantly, it was Christ-like as each piece of his direction was thoroughly bathed in a love that was undeniable and impossible for me not to see.

Dale was a friend. He had much to do given his ministry responsibilities. Dale had a young family and had the task of balancing what was on his plate like all of us. He chose to include me on his list of things that were important. He took his responsibility to me, as my shepherd, seriously. He prayed for me as I had never been prayed for before. He was a constant reminder of God's light. He became a friend; unlike any friend I had ever had before. His words, the resources he placed in my hands, his humor, and his willingness to walk me through the scriptures I needed was, in many ways, what saved my life in every way that I needed to be saved. I told him things that I had only told a few people. I trusted him. We met together every week for nearly seven months. He made it clear that he was available to me day and night, and he did not want me to feel that I was alone on my journey. Once again, God was using someone to be His face, His voice, and His ears in my life. Dale constantly reminded me of Christ and the source of hope that He promises to each of us when we find ourselves in those dark chapters of our lives.

The discipline and accountability afforded to me came at a price for those who were implementing the plan for my recovery. It took time. It took thought. It took sacrifice. It took discipline on their part in keeping me safe from the wolves. They were careful in keeping my progress confidential as some within the church thought that my situation should be an open book for all to read. Some were interested in knowing every detail of my struggle for reasons that I cannot explain. I could not afford the energy to put time into their selfish, ill-intended words and actions. My spiritual warriors continued to do their job in keeping me safe within the church's spiritual haven. My trusted shepherds kept me safe as they stood on watch. For some, it took them going against what others thought the church should be doing or should not be doing, given my situation. It was their love and their dedication to doing what was right in God's eyes that led them to be a part of my path to recovery so effectively. They did not make my situation about them and how it had affected them. It was about me and the reality that I was a soul that would either spend eternity in heaven or hell. They sensed the urgency and eternal value of the situation. They did not view it as an event to be played out for an audience. Their approach with me was discreet and well-meaning. They looked beyond themselves and chose to shine a light on my situation...a light that they wanted to glow much brighter than themselves. They held the light of Christ for me to follow as they helped me find my way. I will forever be grateful to the Wilmington Church of Christ and to their faithful minister, Dale, for playing such an instrumental role in my recovery. While there were many days that I was admittedly reluctant to follow, God was patient and, in His wisdom, gave me the time and space I needed to understand fully and, eventually embrace, the provisions He was making for my life eternally.

I have come into the world as a light, so that no one who believes in me should stay in darkness.

John 12:46

In this scripture, Jesus is not talking about physical darkness. He is talking about personal, spiritual darkness. Everybody has dark days. We all have days when we do not want to get out of bed. We have days when we don't want to face the world and the stress that often comes with it. Most of my depression and darkness was from knowing that each day held a new challenge. I was reminded daily of all I had lost, how weak I had become physically, and knowing that I could not control the flashbacks of the family, home, friends, and career that I had lost. I had jeopardized so much. I had bruised my reputation and tarnished the credibility and trust I had built throughout my career. I now had my work cut out for me in trying to rebuild all that I had lost. The task of completely rebuilding my life seemed impossible, and the process of doing so appeared to be nothing short of exhausting. The overwhelming nature of my situation led to a darkness that is impossible to describe and a hopelessness that, at times, made me physically sick. With the relationships I had established with Dale and leadership at the Wilmington Church of Christ, I knew that I would not need to face the darkness alone.

CHAPTER NINETEEN
Spiritual Darkness

Holding onto Christ should have been my response in my attempt to conquer the darkness of doubt and stress. It was necessary that I did not just find Christ, but that I also find the attributes of Christ that I had not fully understood or had completely over-looked. Living outside of the peace and joy that Christ offers, meant me trying to manage the stress and the difficulties of my life based only on my understanding of what was happening around me.

This inability to discern the various pieces of our lives leads to overwhelming stress. Once stress sets in, it can easily take over and, if left unchecked, stress can cause us to misplace our trust in things that are a temporary fix to problems that need our long-term attention. These temporary, emotional fixes are clever traps that Satan sets to entangle us in a world that is far from the haven of God's love. They are designed to separate us from God and the joy that He wants us to experience. Once you have stepped away from God's light and into darkness, it is next to impossible for you to navigate successfully through life. With each step taken away from God, the path gets more difficult to see, and Satan, just like the wolf waiting for a small calf to wander away from the herd, will attack you when you are least prepared to defend yourself.

There is not one of us who has not lost our way at one point or another. Each of us has had the experience of being lost and overwhelmed. Feeling lost and in the dark creates a sense of being alone. Those feelings are contrary to what God wants for our lives. He wants to be a source of help and encouragement and for each of us to remain on His path. His is a well-lit path and a path leading us to a life of joy and fulfillment.

Unfortunately, stress and all the things I have mentioned will lead us to doubt and, when we begin to doubt ourselves, we begin to question God's ability to love us. When we get to the point of doubting everything and not having the confidence that God can love us in our sinful state, it is easy to begin to think that our lives no longer matter. This is when things can get out of control and go downhill. If this becomes our way of thinking, we can easily slip onto a path of self-destruction.

My path to recovery was shrouded with an occasional dark day. Satan continued to disrupt my mind and heart. I had days when I convinced myself that I had fallen so deep into a dark hole that nothing could salvage my soul. Even though I was surrounded by people expressing genuine love and interest in me, I had moments of doubt and depression. The process of recovery seemed exhausting and impossible to manage. Therefore, I had days when my attitude was that there was no sense in seeking help. It was too late. I was trying to be personable, brave, and outgoing on the outside, but I was alone and withering emotionally on the inside.

> *Then Jesus told them, "You are going to have the light just a little while longer. Walk while you have the light before darkness overtakes you.*
>
> *Whoever walks in the dark does not know where they are going. Believe in the light while you have the light, so that you may become children of light."*
> John 12:35,36

The light that Jesus is talking about here, within this scripture, powerfully shines His presence among us. It is His light that we are to use in finding our way through the dark shadows of this world. As a teenager, I remember being convinced to go to a haunted house with my friends. I despise that sort of thing. I'm not too fond of things jumping out at me unexpectedly, and I have never been a fan of the dark. I remember making my way through the haunted house and clinging to the shirt of the person in front of me while having an overwhelming sense of anxiousness in not knowing what or who was around the next corner. While that experience was just for fun, some live their whole lives in the dark and are thrown off balance by every stressful situation that comes their way. That is not how God wants us to live our lives at all. He wants so much more than that for us. He wants us to see things and people clearly, and His light provides the perspective we need to navigate in life successfully. The lantern of hope is securely planted in His hand. We need only to follow His lead. Be prepared if you are reluctant to follow. Living in darkness means you might grab onto something harmful. If you are like me, when looking for something in the dark, you manage to find everything in the room except for the very thing you need.

CHAPTER TWENTY
Nowhere to Look but Up

Perhaps you are reading this book and have no sign that light of any significance is shining anywhere within your life. Trust me; I know how that feels. You may think that your light has been turned off and with each attempt to get it back on, you are convinced that you are destined to live your life in darkness.

My life became an unpredictable cycle of good days and bad. On the good days, I felt that I could conquer the world. On the bad days, I felt so beat down that getting out of bed was something I could not muster enough mental or physical strength to do. I would become numb to my emotions and the world around me. I felt nothing. I, at times, became void of care, concern, and physical motion. I was paralyzed by fear and doubt, both emotionally and physically.

I have been deprived of peace; I have forgotten what prosperity is.

So, I say, "My splendor is gone and all that I had hoped from the Lord."

I remember my affliction and my wandering, the bitterness and the gall.

I well remember them, and my soul is downcast within me.

Lamentations 3:17-20

Stress can cast a shadow of doubt and discouragement on everything for those who experience it. I know. In my mind, there could not have possibly been a light bright enough to get me back on track. My life had fallen completely apart. Some of the most treasured and important parts of my life were gone, and I sensed that those parts would not be afforded back into my life again. As speculation became my reality, panic set in as I knew that I needed those parts to assemble a framework on which to reconstruct my life. I needed to trust God and be patient.

My journey to recovery would not be easy, and it would take time.

In my moments of depression, I asked myself, "Does anybody really care?" I had convinced myself that no one did. I wanted my journey to be easier than I found it to be. While I did have people who were helping me, some of the truths God was expecting me to learn would need to be discovered on my own. A part of my journey would need to be in me finding aspects of God's truth, and I see now that God knew that if I discovered those things for myself, I would be more likely to take ownership of those truths and hold them tighter and closer to my heart. God, in His wisdom, knows how each of us learns best, and if it means us discovering truth for ourselves, then that will be the path God will choose for our learning experience.

I studied Christian education in college. I remember a professor explaining to our class that it is much better to show students how to discover the truth about something themself, rather than simply telling the student. She referred to it as the "Yellow and Blue Make Green" theory. You can say to the student that yellow and blue make green or let them discover that truth for themself. The illustration she would share in conveying this concept was placing yellow and blue paint in front of a child, allowing them to put their fingers in the paint and mixing them. Of course, as the colors are blended, the student experiences the joy of discovering something new. They discover something extraordinary through the fun and hands-on learning experience of finger painting. I wish the lessons we needed to learn as adults were as easy as knowing that yellow and blue make green. Unfortunately, the lessons we need to learn and make practical application of, are much more involved and complicated. However, the same principle applies.

We must learn by doing. We must engage ourselves and experience life and the helpful lessons that life can bring. God will allow us to experience something painful if it means that we will be more likely to learn, apply and remember the lesson in the future. This experiential learning exercise is not only for our spiritual well-being, but it is also for the sake of the example we can set for others. In the process of learning and maintaining our walk in God's light, we must be mindful that people are watching us. They are watching us closely as to how we, as ones who have professed Christ, deal with the trials and tribulations that life can often bring. I knew that this would undoubtedly be the case for me. I had lived a very public life, and this chapter would be no different. I had an opportunity to teach something of value to those who were watching my attempt to recover spiritually, and I had to convince myself that, if done right, my complete recovery was going to take time and patience. I knew that God could use my situation in a way that could bring Him glory. As we strive to obey Christ and allow His light to guide us, we must maintain an open mind knowing that we can always learn something new about God and ourselves as His children. I knew this to be accurate, but did I have the patience and attitude needed for God to work within my heart?

God often expresses His love for us with discipline and teaches us lessons. This is what fathers do. It is that kind of love and care that sends us a clear message of His love for us as His children. Just as any good father would do, God allows us to experience things that can make us more robust than what we thought possible. Our job is not to let those teaching moments come and go in vain. If we make a mistake, we need to learn from it, and we need to apply the truth we have learned to the next obstacle we face. If we can do that successfully, then our moments of failure will not be in vain. Those moments will make us stronger in our ability to handle adversity for ourselves and to assist others in doing the same. Embrace the teaching moments.

God did not change my circumstances, but He was faithful to keep my heart firmly grounded in Him where I could see His light shining clearly as a means for me to find my way through the difficult circumstances. We make the mistake of confusing the light of Christ with Him swooping in and magically waving a wand and making life's difficulties disappear. Life introduces us to difficult situations and people. Still, with the encouragement that God gives us through His son, Jesus Christ, we can expect and anticipate joy in knowing that He can give us victory over anything that Satan might put in our way. He takes His role as our protector and teacher seriously. Again, as our Father, God wants to protect us. He does not like to see His children get hurt. However, none of the care and protection that God affords to us through His Son, Jesus Christ, comes without a responsibility on our part to seek Him daily. His provisions for our lives must come with a commitment on our part to share His kind, gentle and caring traits, along with the lessons we learn, with others.

As a child, I would adopt ducklings from a local museum of natural science every spring. The ducklings were a day or two old when I received them, and I typically cared for the ducklings for about six or seven weeks until they were old enough to venture out onto our pond and be independent of my protection and care. For me, raising the ducks was a great deal of fun. They adopted me as their protector. They would listen to my voice, follow me from place to place, and learned to depend on me for their food, water, warmth, and overall care. They trusted me to meet their every need as they were far too young to take care of themselves. It amazed me that these tiny ducklings were wise enough to know that they needed to depend on me to thrive and mature. As God's children, we, too, need to take on the attitude and trust of the ducklings that I raised as a child.

We need to listen to God's voice and follow it! How many times have we tried to handle a situation on our own when we should have asked for God's voice to lead the way? I know of many times when I would have been much better off to have just sat still and listened to God and to have allowed Him to lead the way. We need to allow Him time and space to offer solutions to our problems and trust Him to provide the care that He longs to give. When we find and implement the discipline to listen, we need not be surprised when we hear His voice or feel His Spirit gently leading us. And, if you are willing to listen, are you as ready to obey?

Can we learn something from a few baby ducks? You better believe it! Opportunities to learn are present all around us if we pay attention and apply the beautiful truths that God has so faithfully placed before us. Do you know that baby ducks are not born with the ability to repel water? Ducklings can only do that after receiving a special oil on their feathers that they get from the base of their mother's tail. Their oil and ability to repel water come with maturity. God has given us plenty of tools and words of encouragement to repel pain and suffering away from our lives. We need to trust Him and stay beneath His protective wing. I share that because, unlike a duckling's ability to eventually wean itself and step away from a mother's protective care, we will always be children in God's eyes. We will never mature beyond God's wisdom, counsel and protection.

Struggles will come and go, and God wants our character to be strengthened and enhanced in the process of life and ministry. Through our trials and successes, God wants us to become more dependent on Him as we stand under His light and as we become more intentional about the trust, we place in Him. We are much better off to trust Him in His all-knowing wisdom than to be misled and seduced by a world that so carelessly misplaces their trust and well-being in the temporary things of this world.

Even though I walk through the darkest valley, I will fear no evil, for you are with me; your rod and your staff, they comfort me.

Psalms 23:4

It is in the darkest parts of our lives when God's light can shine the brightest, but so many times, in our darkness, we choose to go it alone and never know what a difference Christ could have made. When we are confused about what path we need to take, it needs to be God's light that we allow to guide our steps.

When Jesus spoke again to the people, he said, "I am the light of the world. Whoever follows me will never walk in darkness but will have the light of life."

John 8:12

The difficult circumstances that throw us off track tend to make us doubt ourselves, others, our faith, and our purpose. The doubt that I was experiencing in my life made me wonder if I would ever experience happiness, joy, and love again. Fortunately, I had people guiding me toward the ultimate source of encouragement and help. When you face doubt, there is a reliable source that will never steer you in the wrong direction. The source is God's Word. His words are constantly in place for our benefit so that we might find a light to keep us from stumbling in the dark. God's Word is the only reliable guide for our lives. It is a ray of hope that will shine an understanding on even the darkest of situations. It helps us to see things clearly. It prevents us from bumping into problems that will bring harm and distractions. When we see things clearly in His light, the doubt in our mind and our heart will fade away, giving us a Christ-like attitude in knowing that anything is possible through God, the Father.

I am confident that God used my depression to learn new attitudes, thoughts, and choices that helped me develop a fresh and focused mentality toward a life now centered in Him. He wants us to experience joy abundantly! Not only does He want His light to reflect on your life for your own good, but He wants our example to be a source of hope for others to see as well.

CHAPTER TWENTY-ONE
A Light Named Eleanor

The brightest light of Christ that was consistently shown to me was the light that was ever lit and shining forth from a dear woman named Eleanor. Eleanor was an active and dedicated member of my church growing up. While in middle school, I had the opportunity to have Eleanor as a Sunday School teacher. She was kind, firm, caring, and quite serious about us learning what we needed to know about God and His expectations for our lives. Did I mention she was firm and quite serious? As a 6th grader, I was a tad intimidated by her. Like most children that age, I was immature and did not take her or her class as seriously as I should have. Don't get me wrong. I liked her. I recognized that she was very good at conveying the Word of God, but I was young and had prioritized other things as far more important than learning the golden rule in Sunday School. I had a hard time paying attention in class. At that age, everything struck me as funny and, in my attempt to get attention, I would act up, distracting the others in the class. There were many times I had to be separated from the class, and on one Sunday morning, Eleanor pointed out to my buddy and me that we were the clown and ringmaster of the circus we had created within her classroom.

As frustrated as she would get with me, her light was always shining boldly and brightly for me to see. While her words were firm, her spirit was gentle and loving. She pressed on in setting an excellent example for me of unconditional love and Christ-like dedication. She would send me cards in the mail accompanied by notes of encouragement telling me what a fine young man I was and how God had a plan for me. She would often write about my energy and animated personality and how God could use that for His glory. Eleanor believed in me. She believed that God has a plan for everyone, and each of us has a responsibility to surrender to Him and find His purpose for our lives. She never failed to hold God's light up for our wayward Sunday School class.

As I matured and moved beyond her class, she continued to encourage and love me. The notes in the mail kept coming even through college. I would go to my mailbox, and there would be a card and a few bucks from Eleanor. The note always contained the same message. It was a message of hope and a reminder that God had a plan for me. I still have, and use daily, the engraved letter opener that Eleanor gave me as a college graduation gift. Upon my college graduation, she continued to be a source of encouragement to my young family and me. She would shower us with gifts and would constantly let me know that she prayed for me, my family, and ministry, and there was no doubt in my mind that she did. She took her God-given responsibility of being His light for others seriously. The light that she shined was welcomed, appreciated, and served as a source of encouragement.

Eleanor was someone I respected. Over the years, she became someone I would never want to hurt or disappoint. Within a few weeks of being out of the hospital the first time, Eleanor, now up in years, frail and feeble, would make yet another effort to shine the light of Christ.

You can only imagine my reaction when my mother came into the family room as I was lying on the couch and told me that Eleanor was on her way to see me. I could not bear the thought of her seeing me in the emotional, physical, and spiritual state that I was in. I was so ashamed. The man she had encouraged me to be, failed and had allowed himself to be taken down by sin. I had not applied the lessons she had taught me. I was a grown man with AIDS, living with my parents, a failure of epic proportions and frail in every regard. She had always seen so much potential in me. I pleaded with my mother to tell Eleanor that a visit was not a good idea. I did not want her to see me like this.

Eleanor was coming for a visit whether I liked it or not. If I was embarrassed, ashamed, or distraught, it did not matter. I would need to own up to what I had done. It might as well have been God Himself coming for a visit.

The knock on the door sent a sick feeling through my stomach. My heart began to race, and my eyes filled with tears. How could I be in the same room with this woman who had done so much for me throughout my life, and how could I look her in the face? I heard my mother greet her at the door, and I could hear her as she made her way to the family room. I began to cry as she came into view. I was barely able to look at her. I lowered my face into my hands and wept only to feel Eleanor sit down beside me and place her hand on my leg. As I turned and looked at her, I immediately noticed a box of donuts in her hands. She said, "Dan (she always called me Dan), you are too thin. I want you to eat these donuts." We both managed to laugh.

The laughter faded, and once again, tears came to my eyes as I looked at this dear shepherd coming to check on her lamb. She was not there to judge me. She did not come to express disappointment, anger, or disgust. She was there to love. She was there to embrace me and let me know that she had been praying for me throughout my hospital stay and that she would continue to pray for me as I recovered. I remember asking her if she knew that I had been diagnosed with HIV. She said, "Yes, Dan, I know." She then proceeded to pull from her purse some articles containing information regarding AIDS and the medical breakthroughs that were being made. She told me that living with AIDS was not what it once was and that people were living long, healthy, and productive lives given the available treatments. This was not the conversation that I was expecting to have with Eleanor, my former Sunday School teacher. She gave me a stern lecture about taking care of myself, the importance of taking my medication, and following my doctor's orders. She assured me that I would be just fine. She told me to surround myself with positive thinking people who would provide support and encouragement to me. Barely able to walk, Eleanor made her way to my home to love me, encourage me, and be the face of God that I so very much needed to see that day. Yes, she spoke of spiritual things that day and quoted scripture, but it was her hand on my knee, the way she held my hand as she prayed for me, and the sincerity I felt in her warm embrace that I needed at that moment. She assured me that I was not alone. She, once again, was a light…a light that offered direction, hope, and peace. Clothed in God's Spirit, she came that day as God's ambassador. Her visit made me feel a sense of direction, and I was able to get a glimpse of a future that was potentially filled with purpose and a future that I had convinced myself I would not have.

That day and my time with Eleanor was yet another milestone for me. I could choose to live in darkness the rest of my life, or I could choose to continue my journey toward the light that Eleanor had held so high for me to see. Yes, I was flawed and had made my mistakes, but I was reminded that day that my life had been a life of wanting to know God and wanting others to do the same. I had given my life to Him as a child. I had dedicated many years of my adult life to serving the church, and, as frustrating as full-time Christian ministry could be at times, I loved helping others! Even given the distraction of my personal battle, I was reminded of how much I enjoyed loving people and being a source of encouragement in their lives.

God was pressing on with His promise of being incredibly faithful to me as He continued to give me direction and purpose. With each passing day, trusting God was something that I was learning to do, and His faithful people were cheering me on by providing on-going encouragement. Given that my past and my battle were now public, I could now, in my newfound freedom in Christ, minister to people that I would have possibly never been able to reach before. I was in the middle of a tragic chapter within my story. Still, I reminded myself that day, after those few precious moments with Eleanor, that it was just that…one chapter out of an entire book of beautiful people, incredible experiences, and bountiful blessings.

My life story was far more than this tragic chapter. It had been a life of blessings, victories, fascinating people, and experiences that had enabled me to enjoy a lifetime of incredible God-given events. As I recommitted my resolve to work through this chapter, I dedicated myself to be careful not to negate all that God had done in my life and ministry up to this point. He had been so good to me! Most importantly, my life had been a life of God working through me despite my brokenness, and my message now needed to be that He could do the same for others. I was seeing that this dark chapter did not have to be the last in my life's story. There was far more to come, and I was starting to see that my life story's ending would be up to me. With God as my guide and instructor, I could write the rest of the story and create a finale filled with joy, depicting a life of redemption. It was evident that God did not expect me to crawl into a corner and die. He demonstrated that He wanted me to have a life and a life that was abundant with His mercies and grace.

> *I am the gate; whoever enters through me will be saved. They will come in and go out and find pasture.*
>
> *The thief comes only to steal and kill and destroy; I have come that they may have life, and have it to the full.*
>
> John 10:9,10

God's Spirit helped me understand how important it was not to let Satan rob me of what God had created within me. God expected me to live in His light and to continue to be an example for others to follow. I would need to trust Him and take Him at His Word. I was experiencing blessings. God had not turned His back on me, and I was seeing His hand reach out to me as He longed to put me back on my feet and give me life in Him. We all have the same choice to make. We can choose to live in darkness, or we can choose to live in the light of Christ. I was learning to choose light!

I know now that the discipline and energy required to steer clear of darkness is well worth the effort. The consequences of sin will catch up with you. At the initial and painfully public unveiling of my sin, I was angry and resentful that God would allow such harsh and lasting consequences to enter my life. Still, I am grateful that I was allowed to change course. I had carelessly taken the risk of one day standing before God, having kept my sin private and unresolved. I would have stood before God covered in sin and would have found myself pleading for a life of eternity with Him. I can't pretend to know what that picture would have looked like on that day and can't bear to think about how that scenario would have unfolded.

If you live in darkness, trust Him now and allow Him to take the reins of your life from your hands. He is much more capable than you when finding the path you need to follow. He will provide the light for you to do so.

CHAPTER TWENTY-TWO
An Angel to Embrace

With time, I decided to venture back into the world of social media. It was not an easy step as I would undoubtedly be confronted with questions about my circumstances and whereabouts for the past several months. As I attempted to log in, it appeared that my account had been deactivated. With my depleted account were years of documented memories, pictures, posts, and treasured conversations with friends and family. My heart sank. At first, I thought it was just a matter of me not remembering my password, but with time, I realized the account had been cancelled. There was not anything I could do, and, like everything else in my life, I would need to start over, which is precisely what I did. I set up a new account and cautiously reached out to a few trusted friends. Many of my friends responded immediately and were happy to hear that I was alright and greeted me with well-wishes and words of encouragement. Some admitted that they had contacted the church and my family members to inquire about my whereabouts and well-being. Some thought I had passed away. One by one, with those who asked and those I trusted, I shared my story about where I had been over the past several months. Most were sympathetic and offered their support. Some friends and members of my former church became elusive, with some even jumping to the extreme of blocking me from my ability to contact them. I discovered the true definition of "friend" and "unfriend."

Within a week or so, I received a private message. I was so excited at the thought of making a new friend or hearing from an old friend. The message was from Melissa. The same Melissa that had been placed on my heart while I was in the hospital. It gave me chills. I had dismissed the whole "Melissa" experience months earlier from my mind in that it was so odd and out of place in relation to everything else that was going on in my life. Then, out of nowhere, she was checking in on me. I had not seen Melissa for nearly fourteen years (or so I thought) and, while I knew who she was, I could not have picked her out of a crowd.

She identified herself in the message as the woman who had approached me at church following my public confession. I knew then that it was her hug and her smile that had shined so brightly. She was that woman! It was her that had left me feeling like I had been hugged by an angel.

Her message to me was simple. She wrote, "Hey Danny! I just wanted you to know that I have been praying for you. God is good all the time! I would love to share my story with you sometime. I know you may not be ready for that, but let me know if you would ever like to talk. I am praying for peace and contentment for you!" Her message to me had touched me on so many levels. She cared enough to write. She reminded me that God is good. She also mentioned that she too had a story to share, and she told me that she was praying for me. Her message was short, but it said so much. Her simple message ministered to me that day, and I felt as if God was paving yet another layer to assist me in my spiritual and emotional healing.

I responded with, "Thank you for checking in on me, Melissa. I would love to hear your story. Let's get together sooner than later. I think it will help me a great deal to talk to you. My schedule right now is wide open. Thank you so much for taking the time to write me."

She immediately wrote back saying that she was proud of me for deciding to walk in truth. She spoke of the courage I must have had to make a public confession, and she was confident that I was setting an example for others in my honesty and in my desire to seek redemption. She reminded me to focus on the future and keep my eyes fixed on God. "Your joy will return!" she wrote. I started to get a small glimpse of why this woman may have been placed on my heart during my hospital stay. She was going to be a key player in my healing.

Melissa and I made arrangements with the church staff to meet at church one afternoon and talk. Still unable to drive, my parents dropped me off at the church. God's Spirit seemed to pour over each of us as we comfortably shared our stories. We both felt surprisingly at ease, trusting one another with the details of our stories, and God appeared to be giving each of us the blessing of an understanding ear to listen. There were many tears. Melissa served as an amazing source of encouragement as she, in detail, told me how God had partnered with her in her journey to put her life back together after a devastating divorce. Her path had not been easy, but after many years of praying, searching, and trusting God, her path had led her to a place of peace and absolute joy. Her healing was nearly complete, and although it had taken years of trusting and taking complicated steps forward, the peace that she was finally able to grasp was evident as we talked. While our stories were quite different, our spiritual hurdles and challenges were similar.

As the ex-wife of a former preacher and now an active member of the Wilmington Church of Christ, Melissa spoke of how cruel people could be. She told me how her ex-husband had endured the thoughtless and hurtful comments of some within the church they had served when he, too, had fallen prey to temptation and put his career and their marriage in jeopardy several years earlier. To the best of their ability, as a couple, they took steps to press forward in seeking help for him and their marriage and, while people were willing to help, many within the church chose to hate and ignore. We talked about how consequences are all a part of God's warning to us about sin. We discussed the church and the significant and vital role in disciplining and holding members of the body accountable. Still, neither one of us could accept that hate and responses uncharacteristic of God fall anywhere within that process.

Sin met with sin is not in the mix for anyone seeking forgiveness and healing. Melissa and her ex-husband found out how difficult it was to find forgiveness from some they had loved and nurtured within the church they had served. They, too, were left asking the question, "Is this how a lost and dying world views the church?" If so, was it something they wanted ever to be a part of again? She told me of the hate mail from someone within the church. The hate mail only added to the pain that they were already experiencing. It was almost as if some were taking pleasure in seeing a sinner struggle. The church needs to be different. It needs to be better!

I can speak assuredly that hearts should have been breaking given the circumstances. A desperate attempt to love at that moment would have been the correct response by those witnessing their pain. Some chose love while some, within the church, wore the hat of judge and prosecutor, sending a clear message that they were far more capable than God, Himself, to do His job. Our job is to love and assist those who have lost their way. Our human emotions often get in the way of doing the work of God, and it is for that reason that one must be disciplined and ready to display Christ and His character in all situations. Is it easy? I think not. Is it imperative that we learn the ways of Christ regarding

His ability to love, extend mercy and offer His hand of support? Absolutely!

Let me emphasize once again that I am a sinner. My sin destroyed my life and hurt people in ways that I will never know. In an instant, I lost treasured relationships, my career, my home, and my health. I lost everything and had only myself to blame. Each of us must take responsibility for ourselves by partnering with others and God and living our lives the best we can. This is the expectation that I want to convey. It is this truth that I want people, myself included, to understand. When dealing with one another and the reality of sin, people often collide and make life a picture of difficulty and heartbreak, and it is, but Christ offers a path of coping and getting us back on track. We must learn to live life together, affording one another forgiveness, love, and acceptance.

I know the destructive power of sin, and I also know the destructive power of one's inability to love and forgive. Both are just as devastating as the other.

While knowing God's will and instruction for our lives, each of us can fall prey to behaving poorly and into behavior unbecoming of a child of God. I was convicted of making good on what I had experienced throughout my healing process of which, by the way, I am still in. I have learned many lessons, and I continue to maintain an attitude that keeps my mind and heart open to what God might still want to teach me and others through my journey. My eyes have been opened to various truths that I want to share with others. The realities and lessons I share are crucial to all of us as sinners and as individuals who are allowed to love, accept and aid in the healing of those who are struggling. We must become the church, the loving body of believers, and the haven of a safe retreat that God expects us to be. The church must be a place to confess our sins and get the help we need. The world offers enough shackles without the church doing the same. Are we prepared and equipped to be that for one another and for a world that needs Christ?

Melissa and I continued to stay in touch as she became a valuable source of encouragement. She was determined to help me find God in my situation and refused to allow my, sometimes pitiful, attitude to get in the way of God's plan. Melissa was convinced that God had a purpose for my life and prayed with me daily over the phone. She questioned me often about my relationship with God and would call asking for a report on the progress I was making with my Christian counselor and mentor. She asked me tough questions and stretched my mind in figuring out why I had done what I had done and developing safety nets to make sure that it would never happen again. She, at times, spoke frankly to me and would periodically give me reality checks making sure that I understood the severity of the mess I had made. With that, she made sure I knew that there would be blessings to experience and gave me hope in telling me that my life was not over. Melissa, a single mom, and teacher had her plate full enough without worrying about me, but she was passionate about me having the support I needed. It was apparent to both of us that our friendship was something to be treasured. She would come and visit me at my parent's home. I had a new friend in what was now my new life.

We enjoyed talking with one another and eventually figured out through our daily conversations that we were seeing the same Christian counselor. We talked about our individual counseling sessions and the advice and direction we were being given. We made it a point to provide encouragement to one another in each of us making a practical application of the guidance we received. Like teenagers, and unbeknownst to our counselor, we started scheduling our appointments with him strategically so we would have the opportunity to see each other in his office. Our encounters in his office were brief as it was just a simple crossing of our paths as she left and I arrived, but given my life and the low spot I was in, I looked forward to seeing her, if only for a moment. Her countenance, without fail, always shined a light on my day.

Melissa was there for me throughout my journey. She would talk to me about finding a job. She was sure that I would one day have a place of my own, raise the chickens I had enjoyed so much and have a yard and garden to tend. While I listened, I thought she was too optimistic and that she did not see the reality of my situation. Her words were far more significant than her own. Her words were God's words of encouragement speaking through her as she prayerfully sought to be a source of ministry to my heart and mind.

There was no question that she would, on occasion, grow tired of me feeling sorry for myself. There were many conversations that she would point her finger and take a motherly tone as she set me back on track, snapping me out of my frequent "I can't" attitudes. She reminded me that I would one day do all the things I had done before. She was confident that God was working and that I needed to be patient. She was a constant reminder to me that God was far bigger than myself and that He had a plan…a plan that, in time, would come together and bring me the purpose and resolve that I longed to see. She would text me scriptures, send me devotions and Christian music videos. Each was explicitly picked and sent, given whatever struggle she knew I was facing on that day. She reminded me that God's joy would find a way back into my heart, and I would rediscover the person that God had originally designed me to be. She was a voice in my ear telling me that her God was much bigger than the box I was trying to put Him in. She was right. God's blessings continued to far exceed anything I could have possibly imagined.

CHAPTER TWENTY-THREE
Warriors vs. Critics

Was it not Christ who set the example in teaching us that we love the sinner? It was Zaccheus, someone who was despised and who crookedly cheated people out of their hard-earned wages, that Jesus called out and extended an invitation to have dinner. It was the woman caught in adultery that Jesus physically embraced and dared others to ridicule if they were without sin. He extended forgiveness to Peter. Christ loved people. He put himself in the presence of sinners so relationships could be nurtured, and bridges could be built between Him and those who He wanted to experience the love and salvation that God had designed for them. Even as Christ hung on a cross, He extended love, mercy, and grace to the criminals who were hung on each side of Him. Even in death, His focus was on others.

Given my situation, many people stepped into my life and loved me unconditionally. I am also aware that there were some who I had hurt that needed to focus on their own personal healing given everything I had put them through. They needed time and people in their lives to love them. I trust they found the support they needed. I prayed for them daily…more than they will ever know, and I continue to pray for them.

Some of my most prominent prayer warriors and encouragers were criticized for having any connection with me at all. My spiritual and physical caregivers did not seem to care that some criticized them. They knew Christ had experienced the same type of criticism, and they now considered it an honor to be in good company with Christ and the fact that they were given the opportunity to identify with Him. The love, spiritual direction, and discipline they offered were crucial and would be instrumental in me getting back on my feet spiritually. If I were ever to be counted again as a productive member of the army of God, I needed to find redemption, and that would only come through the love, care, and time-consuming efforts of those who were willing to love me.

There was an investment that needed to be made, and there were, thankfully, those who chose to reflect Christ and make the sacrifices necessary to get me spiritually on my feet. My design was to be His son, His child, and a tool to be used in His hand, and thankfully, some people willingly assisted me in reconditioning my heart and mind to get me aligned with God and His purpose for my life.

Some people did not seem to give my situation a second thought. They treated me like they always had in the past. I appreciated their interest in making me feel as if all was normal, but it was not. Their apparent attitude of sweeping the sin under the carpet was of concern. I was not the person they thought they knew. I needed accountability. Some people did not care, and I don't mean that in a bad way. They did not care. I was treated as if my sin was none of their business. That attitude was, to some degree, appreciated, but we could not just pretend that all was well. It was not.

Then, of course, there were the people who pretended to care about me only to secure their front-row seat to view my raw, human emotions and to see the ugly truth of what really happened. They were not interested in helping but wanted to "pray" for me and encourage others to do the same while adding their take on what was already a tragic and unimaginable situation. Those people quickly surfaced when the frustration mounted in their disposition, given the fact that I would not share my heart with them. Why should I? Maintaining my spiritual gift of discernment, I sensed that they were only in it for the drama. I had enough drama without them adding to it. They were not as much interested in praying for me as much as they were interested in preying on me.

As I felt the weight of my critics and coupled it with the gravity of what I had done, my emotions became more and more difficult to control. Something that I did in response to the weight of all I was carrying is something that I regret to this day. Not long after my move to my parent's home, my former church had all my files, books, and personal office furnishings delivered to my parent's house. My twenty-three-year ministry was confined to the numerous boxes that sat in my parent's garage. My parents kept encouraging me to go through the boxes, thinking that it would be therapeutic to recall the memories of my ministry as I sorted through my belongings. I knew, however, that the process of doing that would only generate sadness and pain.

The boxes contained years of sermons, notes, lessons I had written, and letters. They also included pictures from youth programs I had directed, church camps I had deaned and served, youth conferences, church programs and trips, and personal notes of encouragement I had received throughout the years. As a youth pastor, I had kept every picture colored and given to me, every school picture, and hand-written note from a child or teenager thanking me for an experience or for something that I had personally brought into their life. The boxes should have served as a pleasant reminder of all the good times I had experienced in ministry and of all the wonderful people that God afforded to me to serve. Instead, the boxes stared at me, reminding me of everything I had jeopardized and of all the people I had disappointed.

One morning, when I felt lonely and hopeless and experienced as much negativity from my critics that my heart could tolerate, I felt the need to remove the reminder that those boxes had become. After all, my critics had made it clear that ministry, in any way, shape, or form, would never be afforded to me again. With a heart and mind full of self-doubt and torment, I reluctantly and tearfully made my way to my parent's fire pit in the back corner of their yard and started a fire as I made plans to burn twenty-three years of treasured keepsakes that, up to that point in my life, had meant so much. The boxes contained many things that I would look at periodically throughout my ministry when I needed to be encouraged and reminded of the lives positively influenced by the ministries I had led or participated in over the years. But, on that day, the files were a dark and painful reminder of the failure I had become. The boxes were too heavy for me to carry, so I moved a few files at a time as I made numerous trips between the garage and the fire pit. My mind was tired, and my body ached with each trip back to the garage. Did I think that by burning the files, the pain of all they were a reminder of would go away? The emotions of doubt that had been planted in my mind by my critics were too much to handle, and I carelessly searched for something I could control. I, tragically, file by file, burned most of what I had collected in notes, sermons, cards, and pictures. I had allowed the negative voice of guilt and shame from my critics to get the best of me instead of placing my feet firmly on the path of God's voice of truth. I regret what I did that day. It was a spontaneous reaction to feelings that I should have handed over to God. Had I been patient and chose to listen only to God's voice, I would still have those cherished keepsakes today.

One afternoon a lady from my former church was placed on my heart. She was not only an active member of my former church who served the congregation in many capacities but was someone that I considered to be a close friend. Given the friendship we shared, and what had transpired in my life, I felt a strong nudge from God to call and ask for forgiveness. This phone call would not be an easy step for me. I knew the hurt and mistrust that I must have created within her heart. But, for that very reason, I was convinced that a phone call needed to be made. I was filled with anxiety as I dialed the phone and waited nervously for her to answer. Upon her answering the phone, I said that I could not imagine what my actions must have done to her given our friendship, but that I was calling to say that I was sorry and that I wanted to ask for her forgiveness. While I did not expect an immediate "your excused and forgiven", what I got was something that I was not prepared for. My request for forgiveness was met with a vile and disturbing response. She scolded me with anger and at an unimaginable level. It shook me to the core. My first thought was to hang up, but if I had collected the courage to call, then my response, also, had to be reflective of the courage and discipline that I could have only obtained from God's Spirit at that moment. I knew that hanging up would destroy my purpose and the well-meaning spirit in which the phone call was being made. I waited for a brief pause in her rant and quickly interjected a reminder of why I had called, and I thanked her for her time and hung up. There were many emotions up to that point that I had experienced from myself and others, but I had not witnessed such unbridled anger toward me as I did on that day.

That phone call reminded me of what sin can do in the life of a person and in the life of those they love. Sin does not build. Sin separates us from God, and it separates us from others. For that very reason, God outlines the perimeters of what is good and what is evil. Separation from Him and others is not something that He wants to be a part of our lives. He longs to protect us from the hurt that separation can cause.

The phone call was also a sad reminder of how selfish we can be when asked to afford love and forgiveness to someone. In our hurt and mistrust, we turn inward, only thinking of ourselves and how sin has touched our small corner of the world. This is natural and is something to consider. Those feelings are worthy of identifying, and we must find the tools to manage those emotions. However, it cannot be the focus of the sin. In the threads of injustice where we are unfairly hurt by sin, we must identify with Christ and understand the injustice He must have experienced as He gave His life for our sins on the cross. In identifying with Him, we are forced to humble ourselves and do as He did... love and forgive. This is not easy, but for the one who professes to be a Christian, it must be a discipline to embrace and practice if we are to fully convey the essence of the love and forgiveness of Jesus Christ.

I had to learn who I could trust. There was no level beneath the level I had fallen. I needed people in my life who were interested in creating and constructing a new person with Christ being re-established as my foundation.

It was with the people who were willing to invest in my recovery that I shared my story. I shared the whole story. I shared details of what I had done and the path of deception I had created. As difficult as it was, telling the details of my sin was necessary in that those who I was trusting with my steps forward needed to trust me. I owed them the truth.

CHAPTER TWENTY-FOUR
My Physical Healing

My physical recovery was getting attention. God was at work on many levels. He used something that most viewed as deplorable and untouchable to bring honor and glory to Him. He was orchestrating a plan. Learning to live with HIV has been a process. My diagnosis was paired with so many other pieces of my life falling apart that it was a year or so before I had room enough emotionally to even think about it. As far as I was concerned, my physical well-being was secondary. Initially, I was too concerned about those I had hurt, for the fact that I had HIV to sink in or matter. Given the meningitis and the initial cognitive impairment it left, I am not sure that I comprehended the seriousness of what HIV would mean for me and the rest of my life until months after my hospitalization.

As my heart and mind began to manage my life's emotional and spiritual facets, HIV slowly started to become my reality. The fact that I had something that there is no cure for became real and frightening. I was also dealing with something that had so many stigmas attached to it. HIV carries with it assumptions and stereotypes. Even as one who was living with it, I, too, had misconceptions. I continue to educate myself on the disease and the research being done to find effective treatments and a cure. I cannot change my diagnosis and therefore have chosen to live my life with HIV as a help, source of encouragement, and warning to others.

My HIV was declared "undetectable within a year," and my immune system continued to strengthen and grow well into the normal range. I, too, was thankfully spared the side effects of the medication. My body tolerated the treatment and was responding accordingly.

In one of my attempts to thank my doctor for all the quality care and attention I had received, the doctor looked me square in the eyes and said, "Danny, do not thank me. There is a hand much greater than my own at work here, and I think we both know whose hand that is. We have never seen anything quite like this before, and you, my friend, are going to be just fine." I will never forget his words to me that day.

Early on in my diagnosis, my doctor told me that there would come a day that I would not even think about having HIV. He was right. With time, excellent medical care, being blessed with an undetectable HIV status, and with an immune system that is well within the normal range, I have learned to live with HIV. I want people to see my life as an example of living with HIV and not dying from it. There is a big difference between the two. As horrible as HIV is, there is a great deal to be said for a positive attitude and surrounding oneself with emotional and spiritual safety nets. My HIV status is not a secret. I want my journey to be one that others can learn from and be encouraged by. I talk openly about my story when appropriate. I want people to be informed and to know that AIDS is something that is real and is not just something that affects the people we hear about on the news in a foreign land. It can touch people who live next door, people we go to school with, people we work with, and people we may worship with on Sunday. HIV can be contracted by actions that the church considers sinful, but the sin, the disease, the stigma, and the people it has infected should be treated and handled with a Christ-like portion of grace and mercy. I must also point out that, for some, AIDS came to them by no fault of their own. They did not ask for it. They did not deserve it. It can be a difficult situation unfairly handed to them through tragic and unfortunate circumstances beyond their ability to control. Be mindful of your words and attitudes toward this disease and the people who carry it. Your love and support can make a huge difference in the life of someone who lives with HIV.

CHAPTER TWENTY-FIVE
Showdown with a Push Mower

I jumped at every opportunity to exercise, optimistically thinking that I would evolve back into the strong, sturdy man I had been before my diagnosis. My sister, Debbie, had a small yard that I volunteered to mow for her once I felt strong enough to do such a chore. Dad dropped me off at her home. Before leaving, he started the mower since I did not have the strength to manage the pull starter. I also knew that if the mower died, this would be problematic as it would mean dad having to come back to start it back up. Once again, I was reminded of how I had taken for granted my health and the ability to manage a simple task within my life. The yard, located at a busy intersection in my hometown, was small, but I was taken back as to how physically excruciating it was for me to mow. I had high hopes of being ready for such an activity.

Mowing and doing yard work was something that I had always enjoyed. I had enthusiastically maintained my yard, and I took a great deal of pride in making sure my yard was far more than just a mowed yard. In my mind, I was creating a masterpiece.

Sadly, within a few minutes of pushing the mower at my sister's home, I realized that completing the job in my current physical condition was going to be nothing short of a miracle. My legs were weak, my eyes could barely see where I had already mowed, and my arms ached so bad that I had to rest the mower's handle against my body using my abdomen, more than my arms, to maneuver the small push mower through the yard. I cried. I was reminded of how sick I was and how much of my strength and muscle tone I had lost. I was exhausted, and at that moment, my emotions got the best of me. Unable to press on physically, I stepped away from the mower, letting it die, and I went to the backyard, sat down and cried. I felt pathetic and worthless, and Satan was convincing me in that moment that I was a poor excuse for a man. I felt so lonely at that moment and wondered if I would ever have the strength or have the resources to obtain and maintain a home of my own ever again. A yard that just a few months ago would have taken me only forty-five minutes to complete was now taking me forever to finish. The fact that I was trying to complete the job at a busy intersection made the task even worse in that I was confident that everyone who drove by knew who I was, what I had done, and the consequences that I was enduring. My imagination ran wild with thoughts of what people were saying about me and my pathetic state as they witnessed me trying to pretend that I could mow a yard. I wanted so bad to be normal again. I wanted to do something that could give me a glimpse of life before my diagnosis. I wanted to be able to say that I had accomplished something, and I wanted to know the feeling of being able to take pride in something, even if it was just a mowed yard.

I was not going to let a yard get the best of me. I was determined to complete the job. I had a goal of mowing that yard, and if it took the last breath that I had in me, I was going to mow that yard and make it beautiful. I walked to the front yard and stared at the mower. I did not dare try to start it in view of others. I knew that trying to start the mower could turn into quite a show, and I was sure that the ratings on that show could quickly turn into an R rating due to language. I did not expect it to go well. I rolled it into the garage to have some privacy in getting it started. I pulled the starter and could only manage to get half the cord's length pulled out of what is needed to start.

On top of that, I could not manage and create enough quickness and momentum needed to start it. I tried again…and again…and again. My frustration turned to anger, and my anger gave way to finding the strength I needed to pull the cord successfully and then to hear the beautiful roar of a running lawnmower. I did it. At that moment, I experienced joy in knowing that I had accomplished something that only a few moments ago had seemed impossible and monumental. This was a small victory, but it was a piece of a much larger picture.

With time, each small piece of my life would gradually come together. I needed to trust God, and I needed to give the healing process time. My healing was not going to come quickly. It was a process that God wanted to walk me through slowly and intentionally, giving me plenty of time to absorb the lessons He wanted me to learn.

I remember going to bed that night and, much like a child, feeling so proud of what I had accomplished with that silly yard. I had to let go of the past. I had to reposition the hurt. I had to manage the depression and anger if I moved forward. That was, no doubt, God's expectation. For me to do anything but to take steps forward was to negate what I had already been through. God was at work, and if I gave up, Satan would get the victory, which was not going to happen on my watch. There was too much at stake. My life in a fishbowl was positioned to make a difference in the lives of those who needed to see a genuine application of God's mercy and provisions. I had to get this right. I sensed something good was going to come out of this tragic ordeal. I could not bear the thought of all this happening and me not being able to shine a light on the lessons learned and the grace that God was giving to me unconditionally. I could not give Satan the satisfaction of seeing me fall on my face and giving in to the harsh reality of my consequences. If I was going to live with the consequences of what I had done, then I wanted my life to be a life well-lived and grateful for God loving me enough to discipline my foolish heart.

> *...being confident of this, that he who began a good work in you will carry it on to completion until the day of Christ Jesus.*
> *Philippians 1:6*

CHAPTER TWENTY-SIX
Didn't See that Coming

I started to experience small moments of feeling that life could be bearable again and not just bearable, but enjoyable. I was learning to laugh, and I allowed myself to recognize and enjoy the blessings around me. I had to let go of the control I longed for and then trust God as He held my hand and walked me down the path that He was paving for my life. My new life was unfamiliar and gave me a great deal of anxiety at times in that nothing would ever entirely be as it had been. I learned to go with the flow and trust that God was leading me to His desired goal. It was a path that I was becoming more and more confident in and, with each step, it became evident that the path He was paving was a path to my healing. I was reminded of the many people within the pages of scriptures that, in this challenging time, could serve me as an example of perseverance.

Therefore, since we are surrounded by such a great cloud of witnesses, let us throw off everything that hinders and the sin that so easily entangles.

And let us run with perseverance the race marked out for us, fixing our eyes on Jesus, the pioneer and perfecter of faith.

For the joy set before him he endured the cross, scorning its shame, and sat down at the right hand of the throne of God.

Consider him who endured such opposition from sinners, so that you will not grow weary and lose heart.

Hebrew 12:1-3

I knew my eyesight was improving, and while meningitis left me color-blind, I felt that I was ready to drive. I cannot explain the frustration you feel as an adult in a situation like this. My limitations gave me a glance and a sympathetic attitude towards those who live their whole lives depending on help from others. It is a humbling experience. You want to be treated like an adult, but those around you know that you are not capable, and, in their kindness, they struggle in finding the words to tell you the truth. In my inability to understand why those caring for me were not permitting me to drive, I grew frustrated and angry.

I was confident that in addition to their doubt in my physical ability, there was also doubt in my ability to stay on track spiritually and to not fall again into destructive behavior. Of course, I shared the same concern. While I had stepped away from that behavior years earlier, I also knew that depression and self-doubt were instrumental in my fall. In my current struggle in dealing with my new reality and inability to see God's big picture for my life, would I be prone to go back to the reckless behavior I had dealt with years earlier? The thought of me falling back into that was terrifying. I can only imagine how frightening it must have been for those who were trying to get me back on my feet.

I continued to drop hints to my parents that I wanted to drive and hoped that soon they would hand over the keys to the car. However, they still saw things that I did not. My motor skills were still sluggish, and my mind was forgetful and distracted at times. Leaving the stove on or not shutting the refrigerator door are a few examples of the things I was called out for. My eyesight, while it had returned, left me color-blind and what sight I did have, did not give me the ability to see contrast. I was also still dealing with the damaged tissue on my cornea, which prevented me from having good peripheral vision. Without regaining the essential skills that I had lost; it would mean that I would never have the independence or ability to drive or be able to manage a place of my own. In the meantime, I kept busy physically and spiritually, relying on God to bring recovery and strength to my heart and mind. With time, He did, and eventually, the car keys were handed over, and I had a slight sense of the independence I wanted. In that my car had been sold months earlier, the vehicle I was given limited access to was my parent's van.

One morning, while browsing a popular social media network, I stumbled upon the fact that it was Melissa's birthday. I sent her a message wishing her a happy birthday, and I asked her if she had plans to celebrate. Her response was immediate, and she indicated that she did not have any plans for the day. I asked her if she would be interested in meeting me for a cup of coffee. Meeting that morning did not work for her schedule, but she said she could meet for lunch at a local fast-food chain. This would be my first social outing in nearly eight months. I was so excited to have plans for something other than a doctor's appointment or a meeting with my minister or counselor. I remember stopping to find a birthday card for her on my way to meet her. I wanted it to be perfect and to reflect the gratitude I had for her and her unconditional friendship. It took nearly an hour to find an appropriate card. Our time together that day was memorable because it was evident to me that Melissa was more than just a friend. She was a tool being used by God. We talked, cried, and encouraged one another as we shared an inexpensive lunch off the dollar menu. My relationship with Melissa continued to grow, and I started to find the confidence to leave the safety of my parent's home. Like a baby bird learning to fly, my flights were short at first and were limited.

With time, our relationship grew into something more than what either one of us had anticipated, and we found ourselves spending more and more time together. It was hard, at first, for me to imagine anyone wanting to spend time with me. It was even more challenging to comprehend that my heart might eventually find a heart that would love me. It was Melissa's heart that found the grace to love me even given what I had told her about my past. Our friendship turned into something more. Defining what it was turning into was not something we were able to do at first. We sensed God was doing something special to bless both of us, but we were cautious not to let our emotions trick us into thinking it was a God thing if it was not. I remember doing a great deal of praying and reading and allowing God to tell me exactly what I was feeling toward this angel of mercy He had placed into my life. Neither one of us could afford to take a step in the wrong direction.

With time, we told Melissa's children, Gavin and Grace, my story. We did not want them to hear a version of my story from anyone else. We were open and honest and educated them about HIV. We also shared my story and diagnosis with her parents. Spending time at Melissa's was enjoyable. It kept me busy. It gave me purpose, and it gave me someone to take care of and a sense of self-worth. I worked in her yard while she was away at work and did things around the house to help out. I would have dinner on the table when she would get home from work. Having lived a very public life as a minister and performer, this chapter appeared as it would be no different as people were taking note of the time I was spending with Melissa and vice versa.

One day, while tending to the flower beds in the front of her home, a lady stopped by and wanted to know if I was Melissa's yard boy. After a chuckle, I explained that Melissa and I were friends, and I was simply helping her out around the house. On another occasion, an older man stopped his car in the street, rolled down his window, and told me that he and others had noticed that I had been spending a lot of time with Melissa. He then said, "She is the princess of this little village. You take good care of her, son!" To that, I answered with a, "Yes, sir!" People were watching, and they did not seem as interested in me as much as they were interested in protecting Melissa's best interest.

As it became apparent to the public that our relationship was growing into something more than just friends, we had to deal with everyone sharing their unsolicited opinions about our relationship. Once again, the church shined bright in the opinion poll, and by no surprise, it was not those who had chosen to be a part of my healing. It was those who mysteriously and magically came out of nowhere to voice their shallow and misguided advice. Fortunately for us, those who were taking their spiritual responsibility to us seriously were the ones who asked us the tough questions and held us accountable given the path we were taking. It was not that we did not care or want advice. We wanted to make sure we were getting sound, scriptural advice from those who had invested in us and our situation personally. Melissa and I did not take our feelings for one another lightly. If anything, our feelings were horrifying to both of us. We tried to ignore what was going on in our hearts, but the feelings were too strong for us to pretend that they did not exist.

As the reality of everything I had lost became undeniably permanent, Melissa spent more and more time escorting me around and incorporating me into her schedule. She was very intentional in keeping my mind busy and focused on the positive things that God was doing in my life. I looked forward to rides in the car and attending Gavin and Grace's weekly marching band competitions. In her excitement to greet someone at one competition, she left me in the bleachers, forgetting that negotiating steps was still not something I could do very well. Stuck and with people waiting behind me to exit, I slowly made my way down the bleachers by myself and without incident. Situations like these were huge victories as I healed physically. Melissa getting me out of my parent's house and into public gave me opportunities to engage in situations that were therapeutic mentally and physically.

As my relationship with Melissa progressed, many cautioned me to keep my feelings for Melissa in check. Many told me to be careful regarding my steps with Melissa in that I was emotionally vulnerable. I, too, was cautious, but it was evident that God's hand was at work. My heart attached itself to the one who loved me with the unconditional love I longed for and needed.

One day, in so many words, my mother asked me if I was falling in love with Melissa. I responded accordingly. While Melissa and I had talked seriously about our future, I was not in any position financially to look too far into the future. I had minimal income, and a ring to signify my feelings for Melissa was not, by far, a financial priority or, for that matter, a possibility. A few days later, Mom called me to the kitchen where she had displayed four of my grandmother's diamond rings. My grandmother, which I thought the world of, loved her jewelry and, in her death, had left her jewelry to my mother. The rings were beautiful and were rings that I was familiar with in that Grandma had worn them frequently. Mom said, "I want you to pick out a ring to give to Melissa." Knowing the rings' monetary and sentimental value, I was taken back with emotion and knew that God, once again, was giving me signs of forgiveness and redemption. He gave me a picture of His provisions with each step forward. Pinching myself to make sure this was not something I was imagining; I reluctantly but gratefully selected a ring to give to Melissa.

Did I dare propose to Melissa with no prospects for a job in sight? Was all this too soon? I wasn't even sure that I was going to make a complete physical recovery at that point in my healing. Was this disease and the emotions attached to it something that I wanted to saddle her with? I did not have medical insurance, and I was broke. Would people question my motives? I worried how an engagement to Melissa might appear to some, but I was quickly reminded that God's Spirit was leading me, and that is the lead that I would follow.

With her parent's permission and blessing, I made plans to ask Melissa to marry me. Jobless and all, I took steps forward in making Melissa, my wife. I was out of control, I had no plan, nothing made sense, and it was one of the craziest things that I have ever done. It was wonderful! I was learning what was important in life and what was not, and I pondered, at times, why it had taken me so long to learn this valuable lesson. Again, given my battle, I had sacrificed so much in mismanaging my priorities. Sadly, and too late to change the past, I was being reminded of what people and things should have been a priority all along. I was learning to trust God. God had taken care of me up to this point, and I had no reason to believe that He was not going to carry me to the finish line. I had to trust God as I had never trusted

Him before.

I secretively made plans with Melissa's school administrators to go to her school and involve her kindergarten class with my marriage proposal. The school's administrative assistant and principal were involved, and the stage was set for a unique and memorable proposal. Melissa deserved the best, and she had waited a long time for love to come knocking on her door once again! She had waited for this moment for nearly sixteen years as she faithfully served as a single mom and had hoped to find her happily-ever-after. Now, understand, I know that I was not exactly prince charming riding in on a white stallion. I was flawed, broken, and carrying with me some heavy baggage, but the cool thing was that she had allowed me to reveal my heart to her. She was taking me for who and what I was. There were no secrets from the start, and it was from that starting line that we would press toward the goal of a life together, centered in Christ. For weeks, I worked out the details of the engagement proposal, and I was determined to pull off a surprise.

I could barely sleep the night before the engagement with great anticipation of pulling off the proposal. That night, as we slept, snow blanketed Clinton County. Melissa enthusiastically contacted me early the following morning, telling me that school was canceled due to snow. My heart sank. She had no idea what this meant. This was horrible news for me, and it was a Friday. Should I wait until the following week, or should I come up with a plan B? I decided on plan B.

Melissa made plans to take me out that evening for dinner. I had spent the afternoon at her home, and as we were getting ready to go out, I decided I would propose to her that night, but how? I spontaneously decided to pretend to be sick but not too ill to go out. I was slow in getting dressed. She, having bought into thinking that I was not feeling well, went out to the car to warm it up and waited for me to finish getting ready. Perfect! I grabbed the ring, got down on one knee in her bedroom, and called her cell phone, telling her I was sick and needed her to come back into the house. As she made her way to the top of the stairs, she was able to see me, the ring, and the sign I had made for her kindergarten students to hold. "Will You Marry Me?" was the question as spelled out on the poster board, and it was met with a resounding, "Yes!" We were married a few months later.

CHAPTER TWENTY-SEVEN
Employment and a Reality Check

I decided that I was physically and mentally ready to take on a full-time job, and I began my job search. Months of searching went by with no prospects of a job. Jobs were offered, but I wanted something that I would enjoy and be passionate about. I also knew that I wanted a job that would lend itself to becoming a long-term career. There were days when I felt as if an employment opportunity was right around the corner, and other days were filled with doubt and me having no desire to even look for a job given my lack of confidence.

My goal was to work within the realm of admissions at a college or university. I had been introduced to this line of work while in college, and it was always something that I felt led to explore. Even in my many years of ministry, I often contemplated making a move to work within the world of higher education. Fortunately for me, I was now located in an area with numerous colleges and universities within a commuting range and one, Wilmington College, within 10 miles of my home. Given my love for people, I knew that admission work would allow me to work with students and their families and work within an environment where I could have a sense of community and family that many colleges enjoy. Melissa became a part of my job search process. She checked college websites regularly, looking for an opportunity that would match my skill set and one that would afford me professional responsibilities that I would enjoy. In her search one day, Melissa discovered that her alma mater, Wilmington College, was looking for an admission counselor. I had grown up in Wilmington and was familiar with the college in that, as a child, I had participated in a youth soccer program the college had hosted and, as a young adult, I had performed in several of their community theatre productions. The job posting, and the responsibilities described, seemed like something I would enjoy, and it appeared to be something that, given my skill set and professional experience, I could manage and embrace long-term. I prepared my resume and cover letter and kept my fingers crossed that I would get called for an interview. I was confident that if I could land an interview, I could get the job.

I received a phone call, and an invite for an initial interview with the Wilmington College Office of Admission. The path for a potential job was being paved. My first interview was with the Director and the Associate Director of Admission. After the introductions, the Director stated that my resume attracted their attention, but given my "lack of experience in admission work" specifically, I was plan "B." Plan "B"? Really? What kind of comment was that? From that point forward, I was determined to help the Director of Admission understand how my years in ministry could easily be applied to the people, organizational and communication skills needed to work within enrollment management at a college. I felt that the interview went well, and a few days later, I was asked to come back with a prepared admission presentation to present to a larger group who would also have a say in who they would eventually hire. Speaking publicly and making a presentation was something I had been doing for years. If I could research college admission and financial aid, put it in the form of a presentation, and convince them that I knew what I was talking about, I was confident that I could get the job.

My presentation and a second interview with the college went well. I did the best I could. I now had to be patient in waiting for a phone call. I had also been told that others were being interviewed and being considered for the same position. As I waited on the call, threads of doubt once again entered my mind. With each day of waiting for that phone call, my confidence became more and more shattered. I had done well, but Satan convinced me that the phone call would not come, and within a few days, I slipped into a state of feeling sorry for myself and wondering if I would ever be able to land a profession that I could be enthusiastic about. The professional and personal confidence I once had was now depleted by my self-doubt and inability to remember that God had brought me this far and He would assist me in getting a job.

One afternoon, after about a week of not hearing from Wilmington College, feeling sorry for myself, I curled up on the sofa with Harley, our dog. I was lamenting to him about my jobless situation. The phone rang. It was Wilmington College. Was it a "thank you for your interest, but we have offered the job to someone else" call or was it the call I had been waiting for? I was greeted by the kind and heartfelt voice of the Wilmington College Director of Admission, Tina Garland. She was enthusiastically offering me a job. She will never know what that phone call meant to me. This was a massive step for me! I started my new career within a week of her phone call.

God was taking care of me once again. I did not just get a job. I landed a job that I really wanted and a job that I knew I would enjoy. It was a job that I could make into a career by serving an institution that I had come to love and appreciate through the years.

Then Jesus said to his disciples: "Therefore I tell you, do not worry about your life, what you will eat; or about your body, what you will wear.

For life is more than food, and the body more than clothes. Consider the ravens: They do not sow or reap, they have no storeroom or barn; yet God feeds them. And how much more valuable you are than birds!

Who of you by worrying can add a single hour to your life? Since you cannot do this very little thing, why do you worry about the rest?

"Consider how the wildflowers grow. They do not labor or spin. Yet I tell you, not even Solomon in all his splendor was dressed like one of these.

If that is how God clothes the grass of the field, which is here today, and tomorrow is thrown into the fire, how much more will he clothe you - you of little faith!

And do not set your heart on what you will eat or drink; do not worry about it. For the pagan world runs after all such things, and your Father knows that you need them.

But seek his kingdom, and these things will be given to you as well.

Luke 12:22-31

God showed me that I was of value and that I meant something to Him. My new colleagues at Wilmington College quickly became more than just co-workers. They became family. Getting back into a routine of working was not easy. It was exhausting for me both physically and mentally. I found myself in an environment different from the church setting I had worked within for nearly twenty-four years. I found it to be refreshing. People were genuine, and within a few days, it was apparent that I had landed in a safe place. It was a place where people cared for me and where people were interested in me personally and professionally. With time, I built trusted relationships with those I worked with and was eventually able to tell my story. It took a great deal of disciplined to mask the emotions of what I was dealing with personally. I tried to maintain professionalism, stay focused on the tasks of what the job called me to do, and strategically position myself as a valued player on the admission team. It was a new world for me professionally. I was learning the admission piece of higher education and all the facets of financial aid and the broader realm of enrollment management. With time, opportunities for professional advancement came.

I was taken back one day unexpectedly by a friend and co-worker at work who, at that point in our relationship, had no idea that I was living with HIV. We were working together managing a booth at a convention when we began talking about the importance of washing hands and how handwashing prevents the spread of bacteria and viruses. As we spoke on the subject, I noticed a tissue that someone had dropped on the floor in front of our booth, and I proceeded to pick it up and throw it away. In disgust and a joking manner, my friend said, "What if the person who dropped that tissue has "The Hiv"? I asked her to repeat what she had said. "The Hiv," she repeated, "You know, HIV…AIDS!" "Oh," I sheepishly replied, having never heard HIV referred to as the "Hiv." My emotions were all over the place. I wanted to laugh and cry, realizing now, for the first time since being diagnosed, that HIV and the people who have it are regarded, by some, as untouchable. It broke my heart, and the experience immediately taught me a lesson about being sensitive to such things and the importance of being mindful that we have no way of knowing the shoes that someone may be walking in.

My friend had no idea what she had done. It was the first time that I was forced to deal with the stigma that comes with HIV, and I realized that I would need to prepare myself to deal with the sometimes thoughtless and careless attitudes toward those who have it. Several months later, I talked to my friend and told her about my HIV status. I also brought up what she had said to me at the convention. She was brought to tears when she realized what she had done and was sincerely apologetic. I assured her that I knew it was not intentional and I was not asking for an apology. I shared with her what I had to come to terms with that day and thought there was a nugget of wisdom we both could take from that experience. I was thankful that I was given an exercise in dealing with those types of comments. It was not the last time that I heard an irresponsible comment about HIV. We both learned a great deal through that experience, and it was a time of growth for both of us when it came to dealing with people and not always knowing their stories.

While my friend's comment that day did upset me to some degree, it has also served me as a lesson in being more sensitive to people. None of us know what is going on in the lives of those we come in contact with on a daily basis. We see attitudes, behaviors, and actions and are quick to jump to conclusions and judgment. What we need to do is to take the time to ask the question, "What might be going on in that person's life that is making them act the way they are, and what can I do to help?" My experience with people is that if they sense you are genuine in your question, they will tell you, in detail, about how they are doing. It might be a stranger, but if they recognize a heart that cares and an ear that is willing to listen, they will gladly share their story. Why? With all the devices we have to entertain, preoccupy and keep our minds busy, people are still in need of people. It all goes right back to God using His children to be His face and voice in the lives of those who need the love and acceptance that He wants them to experience. The question is, "Are we willing and equipped to be the face and voice of God?"

I rejoice in the good news I have been blessed with physically, but I still live with the emotional pain that my sin brought for my family and me. You can't take a pill to cure that type of suffering. It has been an uphill climb, and I have learned who I can trust and to know that there will always be those who are waiting in the wings to criticize. I realize now that it is not necessarily me who is being questioned. It is God.

Those who are standing in judgment are seemingly struggling with forgiveness, grace, and mercy and their understanding of the gift that is given, by God, for all people. Some have a difficult time believing that God can and will do what He has promised us within the pages of His Word. I, too, did not understand it until I experienced it first-hand. Simply accepting it and not thinking that I need to fully understand it has brought me, on many days, a portion of peace and joy. It is a gift that is hard to get your mind around. It is a gift we do not deserve, but it is a gift that we are predestined to receive given God's love for each of us. It is not up to us to understand it. We need only to embrace it, and, for me, doing that, at times, is easier said than done.

CHAPTER TWENTY-EIGHT
Signs of Redemption

A big part of my struggle was thinking that I did not deserve to be forgiven or experience redemption. I had difficulty believing that God would spend time and energy trying to restore me. I had been beaten down so low that I could not imagine making a positive contribution to anyone or anything. I was too tarnished by sin. After all, there were more important things that needed God's attention. Good people were dying of cancer. Some families were being devastated by unemployment. People were dealing with poverty, disease, and persecution worldwide. They needed God. I did not want to waste God's time dealing with something that I had brought on myself.

Fortunately for me, I had people who helped me discern what was taking place in my life. I had never gone through anything like this before. As hard as I tried to stay focused on all that was good, there were too many distractions. There were big distractions that demanded my attention. I wanted to believe that I would be redeemed and restored, but how could I be sure? If I was experiencing true restoration, could I be used in assisting others in their path toward being restored? What did that look like for me and others? What would that feel like? I believed God could restore, but how? How does God restore something wholly broken and not just broken, but shattered into pieces? How could He bring order, peace, and restoration into a life that was totally fractured and destroyed by sin?

Restore us to yourself, Lord, that we may return; renew our days as of old unless you have utterly rejected us and are angry with us beyond measure.

Lamentations 5:21,22

How does one return to God and experience the joy of really knowing Him after going through something as destructive as my situation, and, a bigger question, is it even possible? I could not imagine being renewed and restored, given the guilt and depression I was continuing to feel. Without accepting His forgiveness and ability to restore me fully, my heart would be too distracted by my past to serve effectively within His plan for my life. Could I trust Him enough to receive His grace? Did I really believe that He was able to restore my life and offer me redemption? It was a trust issue. I had to trust Him if I were to move forward and if I were to enjoy the blessings of forgiveness. I could not live somewhere between forgiveness and condemnation. It had to be all or nothing if I were to find the peace and joy God was willing to offer to my heart and mind. I had to either believe that Christ sacrificially died for me and my sins or that His death was simply a man who was crucified by those who hated Him and whose sacrifice meant nothing for me personally. In faith, I had to make a practical application of what I had believed all my life and had encouraged so many others to believe as well. His death was for me. God gave His Son as a sacrifice on my behalf. I needed to take God at His word and know that my restoration was important to Him and that in His amazing ability to be all-powerful and all-knowing, He could transform me into something new. Scripture reminded me that I would not be the first.

Throughout my journey, I have found accounts of faithful men and women throughout the pages of the Bible that, if only for a moment, stepped away from God and then experienced His grace, redemption, and restoration as He carefully and lovingly brought them back to Him. Their stories are shared within the pages of His Word. Their stories portray hearts and minds, like mine, who proved themselves to be flawed, and yet at the same time, they desired to be a part of God's plan for their lives.

In Mark, chapter 14, the Bible tells us the story of Peter, one of Christ's disciples. It depicts Peter's denial of Jesus on the night that Jesus was betrayed and arrested. In the story, we have an example of someone who, again, if only for a moment, separated himself from God so that he could selfishly serve his own interests. Peter, who played a significant role in building the early church, stepped far from the course that Jesus had paved for his life and ministry. In his flawed human state, he turned away from what God wanted to do in his life. However, God continued to show unconditional love and forgiveness and, eventually, restored Peter.

Scripture tells us that Jesus was in the upper room with His disciples. They, together, had participated in the tradition of Passover. During the fellowship, Jesus told the men that one of them who shared with Him in the meal would betray and turn Him over to the ones who would, later that night, arrest Him. As you can imagine, one by one, each of the disciples declared that such a thing would be beyond anything that any one of them would ever consider doing. Peter told Jesus that even if he had to die for Him, that he would stand with Him until the end. Not surprisingly, the story played out just as Jesus predicted it would. Peter denied knowing Jesus and not only once, but three times. When Peter was asked if he was a follower of Christ, Peter said, "I don't know this man you are talking about." His immediate response suggests that little thought or time was given in him, putting into play his denial. In a matter of a few seconds, Peter separated Himself from Jesus. In his decision to deny Christ, Peter stepped out of the light that Christ had so graciously shared with him and stepped onto a path of darkness. Unfortunately, if we are honest, His response is reflective of our nature, at times, when we lean toward a tendency to protect ourselves even if it means denying the One who sacrificed everything on our behalf.

Reading the story of Peter's denial is reflective of my own thoughtless and quick response to fall into temptation. My decision to step away from Christ, if only for a moment, was not pre-meditated but was a spontaneous and selfish denial of the One who had given me everything. My decision at that moment, pushed Christ aside to make room for something that would only bring darkness and hurt into my world. Fortunately, in our times of stepping away from God into darkness, He is consistent in His faithful response to bring us back into His fold.

Therefore, there is now no condemnation for those who are in Christ Jesus, because through Christ Jesus the law of the Spirit who gives life has set you free from the law of sin and death.

For what the law was powerless to do because it was weakened by the flesh, God did by sending his own Son in the likeness of sinful flesh to be a sin offering.

And so he condemned sin in the flesh, in order that the righteous requirement of the law might be fully met in us, who do not live according to the flesh but according to the Spirit.

Roman 8:1-4

Paul reminds us in this scripture that there is no condemnation for those in Christ Jesus. This is not a promise for just anyone. It is not saying that we can do whatever we want in life and that there will not be any condemnation or consequence. The scripture is not to be taken as permission to sin. The message here is for those who have accepted Christ and are experiencing a relationship with Him. It is for those who have declared Christ as King and who have entered God's promise and plan of a saving relationship with Him made possible through the sacrifice of His Son, Jesus Christ. The opportunity for us to enjoy the blessings of God's forgiveness comes at a high and personal price paid by God. The grace that God offers to us through that sacrifice affords us freedom from the chains of sin that we place on ourselves when choosing to step out of obedience and onto a pathway of uncertainty and darkness.

Being restored in our relationship with God by His abundant mercy and grace does not mean that our sin will be without consequences. Consequences are not to be confused with forgiveness. We can be forgiven entirely but still required to deal with the results of our sin. God must follow through with the consequences that He has warned us about. Some ask the question, "How can a merciful God follow through with consequences that bring pain into the lives of those He loves and to those that He has adopted as His children?" In His care and love, God has told us in His Word that there would be consequences for disobedience. For God to give us stern warning and then for Him not to follow through with those consequences would strip away His credibility. If that facet of God's character can be discredited, then that discredits His character as a whole and, with that, discredits the entire Bible. God adheres to the instructions and promises that He has given to us. That is what makes Him the terrific and honored Father that He is. He can be trusted. Keeping His word, and maintaining His integrity, is at the very core of God's character.

I do not resent the consequences of my actions. Those who know me and have had conversations with me regarding my consequences know this to be true. While I do not openly discuss the details of the sin I committed, I discuss the implications. While I have, at times, questioned the severity of the sentence that was handed down to me, I accept the consequences and have learned to accept the familiar saying that "Father knows best." I must associate each consequence with God's unfailing and unconditional love for me. He kept His word. He did, indeed, follow through with the consequences of me breaking the rules.

This, oddly, is reassuring and comforting as I move forward. His love and discipline demonstrate His steadfast faithfulness to me. This has not been an easy attitude to embrace, but it is a truth that I have learned and credit to His deep love and concern for me.

My misguided disobedience caught up with me. Our consequences may be immediate and swift, or they may be experienced, as in my case, down the road and far removed from the time and place of the sin itself. My consequences were by no means immediate. Even in me positively taking steps forward for several years before my illness and putting my sin behind me, God was faithful in being the credible father He is by making sure I suffered the consequences for my actions. There were lessons that, through consequences, God wanted to teach and, not only for me but for others as they witnessed my consequences unfold. From the moment of my diagnosis, I did not want my story and the lessons I have learned throughout my journey to be in vain. This is the reason I have chosen to share my story.

Given what I had done and what I had put so many innocent people through, it was hard for me to understand why God would not disown me. For years I preached about the destructive nature of sin and how we, as a society and as a church, must be careful about elevating certain sins over others. This is a game we play. We categorize sin. We have some sins labeled as big sins and some as little sins. With my sin and consequences, I found myself doing the same thing. I had sinned before and accepted forgiveness. Why could I not allow God to forgive me for this sin? I had elevated my sin to be the sin of all sins and to be unforgivable.

As I continued my meetings with my minister and my Christian counselor, it finally began to sink in that God loves me unconditionally. Reading scripture became everything to me. The Bible became a living and immediate application of hope for my life. I was consumed with finding out how a perfect God could love me, a sinner. The answer to that question never came as far as how. What I did come to understand was that He loves me unconditionally and how He does it is something that I may never understand. We need only to know that He does. We must trust Him in His promises to us. Knowing that He loves us unconditionally is part of the blessing that He wants us to experience. He does not want us to be concerned with how or with why. He loves us, and He wants us to partner with Him in ministry and in the joy of bringing others to Him. Again, it is a trust thing. I had to trust that He loves me unconditionally. That is all I needed to know and believe.

We need to then couple that truth with respect and appreciation for all that He is willing to do for us and, with that truth in place, we should unquestionably follow His lead as He calls us to be obedient to His instructions for our lives.

God does not put conditions on the love He chooses to extend. He does not say He will love us if we are obedient. He loves us because He wants what is best for us as His children. I think that it is difficult for us to understand in that we, unfortunately, are often conditioned to love somebody or something because of what might be in it for us. God thinks nothing of Himself. Yes, His expectations for us as His children are enormous and take discipline, but when we come up short, we need not worry that God will stop loving us. With His plan of salvation firmly in place, Christ's blood is more than enough for us to find forgiveness and to be afforded the second chance that many of us need in life.

Because of the Lord's great love, we are not consumed, for his compassions never fail.

They are new every morning; great is your faithfulness.

I say to myself, "The Lord is my portion; therefore I will wait for him."

The Lord is good to those whose hope is in him, to the one who seeks him; it is good to wait quietly for the salvation of the Lord.

Lamentations 3:22-26

I have come to understand that no matter how many times I find myself returning to fill my emotional and spiritual plate, God will be there with open arms and a willingness to love me. My story is not one of having reached perfection in my relationship with God. It is a story of understanding God's character and His longing to fill the voids we have and, most importantly, His want and ability to forgive. In the forgiveness we receive, the burden of guilt and shame is lifted, giving us the focus and renewed purpose to press forward in life. I caution all of us in being tempted to use God's unconditional love and forgiveness as a crutch. God sees our hearts and our desire to know Him. God's unconditional love is always coupled with a portion of accountability, discipline, and consequences. All of which, while difficult to understand, is for our good. He loves us enough to teach us lessons and make us more robust through the trials we experience.

God's unconditional love extends to us the opportunity to heal and be restored and transformed into what we are originally designed to be. He wants to fix us. Even in my broken and dysfunctional state, I managed to maintain an ever-present knowledge of His desire to repair and repurpose me for something good. God sees the broken pieces of our lives and, if we surrender to His leading and hand the fractured pieces of our lives over to Him, He faithfully steps up to the drawing board and designs a plan for a renovation project within our heart. It requires time and patience on His part. God is loving and kind. He waits for us to turn to Him and ask for His help. At that moment, God becomes the architect of our hearts. He works on providing a new foundation and framework for our new life in Him. While He serves as the project manager for our new life, He also serves as the One who is willing to make the investment in our lives. His investment is evident in Him having sent Christ to die for our sins. His investment is substantial. What return are you giving God for the investment that He has made in you?

So, let us get back to Peter's story in the Book of Mark. The Bible tells us that on the morning following Christ's resurrection when the women went to the tomb, they found the stone that had blocked the tomb entrance, rolled away, and an angel was sitting on it. The angel said, "He is not here. He is in heaven." "Go tell His disciples and Peter." Jesus knew that Peter was devastated by his denial. He also knew that Peter was ashamed of what He had done. Peter, no doubt, thought that he could never face Jesus Christ again for what he had done. Jesus, through the instruction to the women from the angel, is wanting to make sure that Peter is aware of the good news about His resurrection. Again, the words of encouragement were, "Go tell His disciples and Peter." Already, a plan is being put into place to help lift the burden of Peter's shame and guilt. The message was clear, and that message was one of assuring Peter that all was well, and all is forgiven. That is just one example of the thoughtful and generous grace of Jesus Christ. In Jesus getting word of the resurrection to Peter, Christ is extending an invitation for Peter to come back to the One who created him and who longed to restore him through grace so that Peter could experience joy once again in life and ministry.

In the Book of John, chapter 21, we read the account of Jesus having a conversation with Peter on the Sea of Galilee's shore. This is His first encounter with Peter following Peter's denial of Him. Jesus said to Peter, "Do you love me?" Peter said, "You know, Lord, I love you." Jesus said, "Peter, do you really, really love me?" Peter said a second time, "Lord,

You know I love you." And Jesus said a third time, "Peter, do you really love Me." Peter said, "You know Lord, I love you."

Jesus, in a way that beautifully demonstrates His impactful method of teaching, was now giving Peter three opportunities to affirm the very thing that he had denied three times before. Jesus is giving back something to Peter that, no doubt, Peter thought had been lost forever. It was an opportunity for a mended relationship with Jesus. In your sin, you may think that God has forgotten you, but He has not. He knows that you have fallen away, but He always gives us an avenue to be reminded that He is willing and able to restore us unconditionally.

At times as I tried to imagine how my journey would unfold, I would have never foreseen how God would intervene, orchestrate and weave my life back together. It is one of the most incredible displays of God's grace that I have ever witnessed and, little did I know, that when I did finally discover how beautiful God's ability to restore is, that I would be front and center of an example of restoration that could be shared with others. He took my heart from something lost to something to be used, again, by Him.

Thankfully, I had been encouraged by so many brothers and sisters in Christ to go slow in my healing, to get it right, and to let God take the lead. It is nothing short of amazing as to what God had in store for my life. I have learned to trust Him. The road has been long and difficult given the consequences I live with and some consequences I will live with for the rest of my life. I have learned how to fight back spiritually and emotionally, not by my understanding and strength, but rather by God's eternal guidance and love for me. He faithfully continues to cheer me on as I keep my eyes on making it to the finish line. My restoration's complete results remain to be seen, but I have learned to anticipate additional blessings. Each of us are a work in progress. Our lives are a never-ending process of growing in Him throughout our time on earth, but, for now, my results, unquestionably, are redemption and restoration. The signs of redemption and restoration are undeniable.

I have taken steps in allowing my heart to beat again. My heart, in my AIDS diagnosis, my lengthy illness, recovery, and in dealing with the relationships that I had jeopardized, had grown stale and void of feeling. It was a heart that had grown foreign to me in that the joy that I had tried to hold onto my entire life was gone. It was completely unrecognizable and, in turn, difficult for me to find. The parts of my heart that I could recognize were difficult to interpret. I was unsure how to apply what I felt toward the steps I knew I needed to take toward my spiritual recovery. In not knowing, my heart foundered. My joy had escaped me, and, at times, I was frightened that joy would forever be unattainable. The fear I faced was crippling. It shut down my being and purpose. Void of emotions and caring about anyone or anything, my body, at times, became frozen, and my mind was a space for Satan to place doubt and self-pity within easily, and he did.

I credit Melissa for her ability and persistence in reminding me that I was tragically negating God's ability every time I doubted that I could ever be used by Him again. With her encouragement and with me now starting to see a glimpse of what God was doing in my life, I was able to see the signs of redemption in my life that others were seeing. I had taken accountability for the sin. Moving forward, I needed to learn to be responsible for the life of joy that God wanted me to live. This was the testament I had longed for from the start. My fall was not going to be in vain. My story was being authored to reflect what God was doing regarding Him making an undeserving application of forgiveness for what I had done. God was now showering my life with visible redemption indicators in the form of blessings. I dare not waste the opportunity to boldly, yet humbly, share my story to encourage others as they, too, confront their battles.

My battle has experienced victories that have been layered within it. Those victories are now posing a threat, dangerously so, to Satan and the dark, joyless life that he so very much wants me and others to experience. Through my experience, I have a deep understanding of the words to a song that I had sung so many times as a child. "Onward Christian soldiers, marching as to war!" This has become an honest, heartfelt, and personal battle cry! As one who had felt defeated, I am gaining the strength and courage to pose a severe threat to the enemy and offering to others, through my words and example, the hope and redemptive power of a relationship with Jesus Christ.

> *Therefore, since Christ suffered in his body, arm yourselves also with the same attitude, because whoever suffers in the body is done with sin.*
>
> *As a result, they do not live the rest of their earthly lives for evil human desires, but rather for the will of God.*
>
> *1 Peter 4:1,2*

My tragic story played out in what was nothing short of a physical miracle and a spiritual testimony for others to be encouraged by and to learn from. I had to convince myself to take responsibility for my now redeemed life and carve out intentional opportunities and steps for my new life to bring glory to God. There is no option for me to keep my transformation hidden. I will not allow all that I have gone through to be in vain. I choose to tell my story. I choose to talk openly about my diagnosis and recovery physically and spiritually. God has amazingly taken something shattered and has orchestrated a portrait of hope and a life that is being lived out abundantly so.

CHAPTER TWENTY-NINE
Joy in the Midst of Heartache

If there is one truth I have consistently tried to embrace in life, even in difficult times, it is that we, as God's children, are to be a people of celebration. There are times I have succeeded in doing this and times, as described in the pages of this book, I have failed miserably. We must discipline our hearts to celebrate life daily. Life is a beautiful gift to be enjoyed and treasured and not to be taken for granted. I was ready to walk out on this truth, but God has shown me the reality of true celebration and joy and that each is centered in Him and the blessings He provides. We are to celebrate the positive changes that God has orchestrated within our lives. We need to celebrate lessons learned, even if they surface, and find their way to our hearts during heartache and challenging times. We must celebrate what God is doing through and in the lives of others. We must celebrate the experiences that are shared between family and friends.

God calls us to be a people of celebration! The Psalms tell us that we are to sing for joy, to sing praises with a harp, to sing a new song, to shout for joy, to bless and praise the Lord continually! It is the joy that people need to see within our lives. It is joy that people are looking for, and we have a responsibility to show them what joy, centered within the relationship we share with Jesus Christ, looks like.

Why have we been called to be a people of celebration? Given our relationship with God and the benefits we experience daily as His children, why would we not be joyful people who would want to celebrate life unapologetically? God is majestic, but He longs to hear praises from our hearts. That is a reason to celebrate! God is holy, but He desires to commune and fellowship with us! That is a reason to celebrate! God is all-knowing, yet He wants to hear our thoughts, and He longs to search and know the desires of our hearts. That, too, is a reason to celebrate! I have so many reasons to celebrate my life. I will live with the consequences of my sin for as long as God allows me to live in this beautiful world. I cannot change that, and I am not sure I would, if I could, at this point. Would I change it for those I have hurt? Yes. For me, however, God's direction and discipline have changed my life not only here on earth but for eternity. It is what it is, and the consequences have now become small reminders of what could have been. I could have lost sight of my relationship with God altogether. I am grateful for what I have learned about God and the provisions that He longs to make for my life. He is good. Each of us has a great deal to be thankful for, and there is no doubt that each one of us, no matter the trials in our lives, has reason to tip our hat to God and say, "thank you."

We have been given a beautiful gift in the very Son of God, Jesus Christ. We have God's unconditional love, and we have His forgiveness that makes way for us to experience the second chances that many of us need every day. We have reason to celebrate because the gift of eternal life is available to anyone who desires to accept God's plan of salvation for his or her life. Without the opportunity to live with God for eternity, I would have had nothing to live for. My life was done on this earth, but I knew in my heart that I had to hold tight to His hand in allowing Him to pave the way for me to find redemption and in establishing a gateway to be with Him in Heaven forever. Knowing that He would be faithful in holding my hand and knowing that He was not going to give up on me was a reason to celebrate and, for me, as hard as it was, to maintain an attitude of joy throughout my difficult journey.

You see, our attitude of joy is not just about us, but it is also a tool God uses in our lives to attract others to Christ and His church. Do you smell of a sweet, sweet aroma?

But thanks be to God, who always leads us as captives in Christ's triumphal procession and uses us to spread the aroma of the knowledge of him everywhere.

For we are to God the pleasing aroma of Christ among those who are being saved and those who are perishing. To the one we are an aroma that brings death; to the other, an aroma that brings life.

2 Corinthians 2:14-16

I know the aroma of my wife baking cookies, homemade bread, or a cake will attract me to the kitchen. I love the smell of our home on Thanksgiving morning of the turkey that has been roasting all night long. The smell of pancakes, bacon, and eggs on a Saturday morning will always catapult me to the kitchen. The aroma attracts me to the source and allows me to experience the very source of that aroma.

Is your aroma one of joy so that you might be attractive to those who do not know God? Are you attractive, spiritually so, or are you one of those individuals who people constantly avoid because you always see the glass as half empty? As God's children, it is crucial for us to maintain an attitude of joy because life and ministry happen every day. Have you noticed that? There is no way around it. As hard as we may try to avoid it, life happens, and with life comes an array of circumstances and situations that bring happiness, sorrow, sadness, excitement, enthusiasm, anger, mourning, and a host of other emotions that can sometimes catch us off guard. It is essential to be disciplined in allowing God's Spirit to enter our hearts and minds daily because life can be unpredictable. Life can bring disease, pain, dysfunction, divorce, sorrow, and death. When we face difficult times, we need to remember that we can maintain our joy. We must! In these times, people are watching us as individuals and as a church, as they long to witness how we handle life's stresses.

You might be thinking, "I am hurting. How can I possibly maintain my joy when faced with difficulties?" You might be thinking, "You don't know me, and you don't know the kinds of problems that I am dealing with in my life." You are right. I do not. I do know, however, that we must be careful not to confuse joy with happiness. Our happiness is affected by people, circumstances, and situations. Our degree of happiness can vary hour by hour based on what is going on around us. God does not promise us happiness, but He does promise us joy! Joy is a discipline that we must generate within our hearts and protect as we maintain it by our relationship with Jesus Christ. To maintain our joy, we must come before Christ in humility and brokenness and trust Him fully. It is only out of humility and brokenness that God can indeed have His way with us. Be prepared to strive for these characteristics because brokenness and humility rarely feel good. Trust me, I know. Brokenness and humility rarely feel comfortable for anyone. They will make you squirm and will likely make you want to run from God and do your own thing on your terms.

Have you ever asked the question, "Why? Why is this happening to me?" I have learned in life that there may never be an answer to that question. It is quite possible that God is the only one that needs to know the answer to that question. Sometimes He reveals it to us promptly, and sometimes it takes months or even years. At times, He chooses never to reveal the answer, which is always difficult for us, as His children, because we like to think that we are in control. The reality of life and a relationship with God is that we are not in control at all and are simply a tool in the hand of God as He uses us to bring honor and glory to Him. Do not live with an expectation that God owes you an answer to your question of "why me?" This is when our trust must be fully invested in Him. If you are like me, you have, at times, said, "God, use someone else! This ministry is too hard!" God did not promise a life and ministry that would be easy. He did not promise us a smooth, non-eventful road to travel. He determines our purpose. We must surrender to Him. He wants to use us in the lives of others as He reveals to them, through our example, His love and plan of salvation for their lives. Is there a more incredible honor than to be used by God? I think not.

Life is not fair. The journey that Christ was asked to walk on our behalf was, by no means, fair. It was harsh. There were threads of injustice throughout His journey, and we have every reason to believe that we, too, will be called to acts of service that involve every ounce of our being spiritually, emotionally, physically, and relationally. If I had the opportunity to speak to those who were instrumental in starting the early church, I am confident that they would tell me that it was not easy. I am sure that they would tell me the stories of harsh circumstances, how God's calling was not easy, and how things did not seem fair, and that the expectations seemed to be impossible to accomplish. However, I am also very confident that I would hear how the joy of the Lord is what enabled them to get through the difficult times. I would hear stories of blessings, cherished relationships, and renewed hope as God pressed them toward the goal of fulfilling His purpose in the lives of others.

When you go through an episode of brokenness and humility, you begin to identify with the very brokenness and humility of Jesus Christ and how He must have felt when He was being mistreated, judged harshly, and dying on the cross. Whenever you can identify with Christ and can know Him more, even in a state of ruin and heartache, that should give you reason to celebrate! At the core of our purpose is the instruction to know Christ and to gain an understanding of Him and what He purposed for our lives. When you grow in that understanding and take steps toward Christ, there is always reason to celebrate and experience joy. There is nothing more extraordinary on earth than to know Him more.

…and let us run with perseverance the race marked out for us, fixing our eyes on Jesus, the pioneer and perfecter of faith.

For the joy set before him he endured the cross, scorning its shame, and sat down at the right hand of the throne of God.

Hebrews 12:1,2

Paul is telling us to take heart, to be encouraged, and to hold tight to Christ and the powerful example of humility and brokenness that is demonstrated through His ministry, death, and resurrection. The life that we are called into is nothing that Christ himself has not already experienced and lived. We make the mistake of thinking that God is directing us towards a particular goal. He does have specific ideas for our lives, and He guides us towards the purpose He wants us to fulfill. However, I believe that what matters to God is the process of pressing toward those goals and the lessons we learn in our journey. It is within the process of God playing out His purpose in our lives that lessons are learned, and we are given opportunities to make practical applications of those lessons.

The very process of living and managing our lives glorifies God if we do it well. I am not suggesting that our lives need to be perfect, but I am suggesting that it matters how well we manage our lives when we are pulling ourselves up after realizing we are wrong or having fallen to Satan's temptations. It is how well we do when up against the daily grindstones of life and ministry that will speak of our commitment to God and His church. Our ability to rely on God and His ability to help us rise above and conquer heartache and trials is what will genuinely glorify and honor Him.

My son, Brady, was an enthusiastic and committed participant of 4-H as a young man. It is a program for youth that encourages and nurtures responsibility, learning, and life skills. Brady chose to raise market chickens for his 4-H project each year. He cared for his chicks, raised them to maturity to what he felt was a perfect weight, and would then enter them in the county fair with hopes of taking home the Grand Champion Market Chicken blue ribbon. He carefully planned his facilities, feeding strategy, lighting, etc., with the hope of taking the coveted title of Grand Champion. For many years, he would enter his poultry project and, while he always did well, he could never quite reach the honor of Grand Champion. He would then go back to the drawing board and strategically plan how he could do better the following year.

At long last and after many years of trying to achieve his goal, Brady was given the honor of raising the Grand Champion market chickens. We were thrilled and enthusiastically celebrated Brady's victory! As a dad, I celebrated his victory. He had achieved his goal. He had reached his prize. But for me, I think I was more proud of the process Brady had pressed through year after year as he suffered defeat, learned the hard lessons of hard work with no payoff, and managed to keep his head up as he convinced himself that eventually, he would reach his desired goal. I was more proud of what he had learned in the process of that experience than him achieving his goal of Grand Champion. As a dad, I was excited about what Brady had learned. I was proud that he had not given up on his goal. He stuck with it, applied lessons learned, and achieved the prize. The combination of all that coming together is beautiful for a father to stand back and observe in a child's life.

There is no doubt that God, too, is pleased with us in our ability to manage well the process of life. When we miss the mark, God observes us as to how we react and how we apply the lessons we have learned. Again, I imagine He takes a great deal of pride in watching His children grow and mature in our walk with Him and in our journey with others.

Life and ministry can chew you up and spit you out. Life and ministry can introduce you to demanding situations and difficult people and circumstances. They can leave you bruised and wounded, or the trials and tribulations of life and ministry can make you stronger and wiser. It is all a matter of attitude as to which side you will fall on. Will you be chewed up and spit out, or will you come out of a problematic situation stronger and wiser? The determining factor that will decide your fate between the two is your attitude. Have you ever found yourself in a situation where, to serve effectively, you had to become humble and broken because the task of the ministry was so beyond anything you thought you could do? I have held infants in Africa who were skin on bone. I have walked through a veterans' hospital in Vietnam that housed bed after bed of men injured by war left with no arms or legs. Their daily existence consisted of lying on their beds with no way to get up, no way to hold a book to their face, and no way for them to care for themselves. I have been the guest at many a dinner table in Poland where families offered me their entire months' worth of food, knowing that their children may go hungry. I have seen children in Haiti who were diseased, hungry, and emotionally spent. I have been mocked and spit upon by people in a London city park as I preached the Word of God. While I use some personal experiences that I have had on foreign mission fields to emphasize my point, you do not need to go beyond the borders of where you live to have the opportunity to apply Christianity to human need and desperation.

CHAPTER THIRTY
A Boy Named Corey

Many summers ago, I volunteered to serve on the faculty for a week of church camp for 1st and 2nd graders. This was typically not an age group that I took great pleasure in serving, but the need for my help was presented, and I reluctantly volunteered to serve. In the dorm that I was assigned to, there was a little boy by the name of Corey. When Corey arrived in my dorm, I introduced myself as "Mr. Danny." I also sensed that Corey was not old enough to be attending camp for this age group. Corey attached himself to me, had lots of questions, and, in general, was a very talkative little boy.

"Mr. Danny, when do we eat?"

"Mr. Danny, when do we swim?"

"Mr. Danny, I can't find my Bible."

"Mr. Danny, I don't know what to wear."

Now, I am thinking, "I have a dorm full of boys for whom I am responsible, and I cannot be putting all of my time and energy into Corey."

"Mr. Danny, I can't fall asleep."

"Mr. Danny, my sheets don't fit my bed."

"Mr. Danny, I am scared."

About an hour into bedtime on the first night of camp, I became challenged to manage my patience with this little boy. Corey was driving me crazy. I knew that I would be spending an entire week with this child. I needed to find an extra portion of patience, and I needed to find it quickly.

"Mr. Danny, can I play with my flashlight?"

"Mr. Danny, I need to go to the bathroom."

"Mr. Danny, I can't find my blanky."

"Mr. Danny, can I sleep with you?"

"Mr. Danny, Mr. Danny, Mr. Danny!" The questions and talking went on and on and on!

As a rule, I do not require much sleep, but early the next morning, exhausted and frustrated, I decided that I would not have another night like I had experienced the night before. I had received very little sleep due to this little boy's inability to leave me alone and let me rest. I made my way to the dean and wanted an explanation of why Corey was permitted to attend camp. Again, I sensed he was not old enough. I was right. I found out that Corey did not meet the age requirement. I told the dean that I was not happy about the situation that I had been given and shared with her that more consideration needed to have been given regarding Corey being allowed to come to camp. I stated that he was a distraction to the other boys and me in the dorm.

The dean explained that Corey and his siblings had been split up a few months before camp, and camp was going to be an opportunity for Corey and his siblings to spend some much-needed time together. I thought that was fine and a nice gesture on behalf of the camp, but I, being the dorm dad, had not been consulted. I felt strongly that the needs of the other campers should have been considered and that provisions should have been put into place to provide me with additional help in the dorm. It did not seem fair that Corey was distracting the other boys and myself from our camping experience. I had to ask the question, "Why me?" I sensed a thread of injustice in this situation.

I managed to get through another night of "Mr. Danny, Mr. Danny, Mr. Danny!" The following day, I got up very early and was shaving at the sink, and I was enjoying a few minutes of peace and quiet before the morning bell awakened the boys. Well, here comes Corey. I said, "Corey, it is very, very early. You need to go back to bed." Corey then said, "It is early. My Grandpa won't even be up this early." I said, "Corey, do you live with your Grandpa?" and he said, "Yes. My daddy was killed, and my momma is in jail." I said, "Corey, I am so sorry to hear that." He then said quickly, "One day, the doorbell rang, and when my daddy answered the door, someone shot and killed him." Then he said, "…and I saw the whole thing." My heart broke for that little boy, and, in an instant, I was humbled in that my woes of having Corey in my dorm were shallow, considering all that this little boy had gone through.

That night at bedtime, Corey started up again with, "Mr. Danny, Mr. Danny, Mr. Danny." Then he said, "Mr. Danny, will you come and rub my back? My daddy rubbed my back to help me fall asleep." With that, I went over and sat on the edge of Corey's bed and rubbed his back. Corey fell asleep, and, at that moment, all the frustration, torment, suffering, and sadness in that little guy's heart seemed to fade quietly. I then discovered what an extraordinary privilege it was for me to be placed in that little boy's life. I was given the honor of sharing the love and peace of Jesus Christ with that little guy that week and how ashamed I was of knowing the initial attitude I had taken with him. I was called to be an ambassador for Christ. And while I was reluctant, the Holy Spirit had His way with me that night. Because as I sat on the side of Corey's bed, rubbing his back, I thought of a scripture that humbled my heart and put everything in perspective.

"The King will reply, 'Truly I tell you, whatever you did for one of the least of these brothers and sisters of mine, you did for me."
Matthew 25:40

That night, a five-year-old boy taught me a lesson about being broken and humble, and he taught me about being a faithful servant of God. Even though I was broken and humbled, I still had my joy because I had learned something about myself, about God and how serving others is not always comfortable or enjoyable. When we learn something about God's love and how He desires, above every desire, to share it with others, we have a great deal of reason to be joyful. When we grow in Christ and in our understanding of who He is, there is reason to be joyful and to celebrate.

CHAPTER THIRTY-ONE
Sharing Joy

Love can be given freely. It does not cost us anything when giving it to others. It is an attitude that we must discipline our hearts to generate. It can be shown in the form of a smile, a hug, a listening ear, a word of encouragement, or a simple act of kindness. It does, however, require us to be mindful of those around us and sensitive to what they may be dealing with in their lives. The joy of the Lord is to be shared through the love and concern we show to others. It must be demonstrated through our lives for others to see and to experience so that they can be touched by it and, in turn, inspired to share it with others. Conveying Christ's love might mean a sacrifice having to be made. It might mean us having to change our schedule or embrace someone or a group of people with whom we are not comfortable.

Let your prayer be that God will make you, mold you, fill you, and use you as He prepares for the next chapter of ministry in your life. We are called to serve people. Life and ministry are processes that can wear you out! So, in the process of life, be sure to take a break!

Be sure to protect your joy by taking a break from routine, by celebrating life, and by celebrating the people around you. Christ wants each of us to have joy. Joy does not come easy. Being joyful is a discipline, and it starts with having a relationship with Christ. It begins with acknowledging Christ, who He is, and what He expects for us and our lives.

So, here I am. I am still kicking physically, emotionally, relationally, and spiritually. No, I am not perfect. Through my challenges, I have learned about people, but more importantly, I have learned so much about God. God's Word is true and, if applied to our lives, it can give us joy and provide us the tools we need to live for Him providing us the ability to be a portrait of who He is for others to see.

We are all met with challenges from time to time. The challenges we face are sometimes anticipated, and some can throw us off guard. Regardless of the challenges, we are called to live lives centered on serving others when possible. We are called to make a difference, and our confidence in serving others can only come in knowing that there is a power greater than ourselves. That power and confidence, of course, comes from God.

The day that I opened my eyes and saw total darkness and realized that I was blind was a dark, dark time in my life, both spiritually and physically. I am constantly reminded of God taking me from that dark moment to where I am now. Today, as I press on, I maintain a resolve not to let the simple, daily difficulties of life get me down. They are nothing compared to what God has already faithfully walked me through. With God, and with the power that He makes available to us through the blood of His Son, Jesus Christ, we must step forward and not allow unpleasant people, circumstances, and situations dictate to us as to how the rest of our day, or life for that matter, will go. We must, in the name of the Lord, pick up stones just as David did in the pages of the Old Testament and face our giants. Our stones must be thrown in faith, with grace, purpose, and intention. As we face our giants with our all-powerful and all-knowing God, they will fall and give us the ability to place our focus back on the joy that God wants for our lives. His promises are not just for today. They are in place for the rest of our lives to enjoy. In addition to that, His promises make provisions for our eternity. Being reminded of that truth, we need to be intentional in putting the petty things of this world behind us and strip them of the power that Satan wants them to have. This is a discipline that we must purposefully maintain.

Through my life and, more specifically, through the ordeal with my sin and HIV, I have learned a great deal about truth, mercy, and grace. I have also learned about people and what they pretend to know and what they pretend not to know. I know that my sin destroyed my life as I knew it, and moving forward, I am committed to moving forward focused on God's truth. I have been able to press on because of that truth. His love and forgiveness have given me the strength and ability to live a life centered in Him and a life where I can continue to be called a child of God confidently. I am aware that some have a problem with me moving on and living a life of joy. I maintain that for me to do anything but that is to negate God and the blessings He has shared.

God is good. My life is seemingly on track. With God's help, I have managed to collect the pieces of my life, the ones I could salvage, and put together a life that is joyful and bearing fruit. Some pieces of my life are missing. I continue to work through the emotional and spiritual process of knowing that those pieces may never be recovered. That process is daily. The missing pieces of my life are a part of the debris field created by the storm of disobedience that I participated in. While some of the pieces of my formal life are lost forever, I trust God to help me find the few pieces that I refuse to give up on. For the pieces that I very much long to find, the search will continue, but I must be careful that my search does not come at the cost of those who have chosen to love me unconditionally. They deserve my attention and focus. With Melissa by my side and with her as a constant source of encouragement, I have pressed on and allowed God to reign victorious as to how He chooses for my life to be defined.

CHAPTER THIRTY-TWO
A Treasured Metaphor for My Journey

A few years ago, Melissa and I had the blessing to visit Belize in Central America. I looked forward to the trip and did not take the opportunity for granted, given the fact that there was a period in my life not so long ago when I wondered if I would ever leave the confines of a hospital bed. While in Belize, we had the opportunity to participate in a guided tour to view the ancient Mayan Ruins. This significant and historical archeological site sits in the country's lush jungles, and the journey involved a two-hour road trip from where our cruise ship was docked. As our tour bus ventured off the main road and proceeded down the narrow back roads toward the ruins, I could only imagine the sights and sounds of what I was about to see and hear. I have traveled worldwide from Europe, Africa, and Asia, and yet, I was like a kid as my thoughts kept going back to how incredibly blessed, I was to have this opportunity. Would the Mayan Ruins look anything like the pictures?

As we made our way through the jungle, I was a tad overwhelmed with emotions as I thought about the fact that just a few years earlier I, and others, had convinced ourselves that my life was over. And now, here I am in Belize. I was healthy, happy, and being given a chance to experience something amazing and something that very few people in their lifetime have an opportunity to experience. As the bus came to a stop, I looked out the window, trying to catch a glimpse of the enormous man-made structures but was informed that we still had a short walk through the jungle to get to the site. As our tour group came into a clearing in the jungle, the Mayan Ruins appeared in a wonderful display of beauty and grandeur. It was breathtaking, and I was filled with wonder as I thought about these magnificent structures being built by the Maya people. It was hot and humid, but the experience was so overwhelming that I could not let the heat distract me from the ancient ruins. We toured the sight, listened to our tour guide, and took numerous pictures.

As our time at the Mayan Ruins concluded, our tour guide pointed out a rustic, and might I add, the steep trail of steps that led to the very top of the most prominent structure. She told the group that for those who were willing and able to make the climb, we were welcomed to make the journey to the top before making our way back to the bus. I, for one, had not traveled that far to see these amazing structures from ground level and then simply go back to the bus. If I was being offered a chance to go to the top, I was going to the top! For me to have not climbed the ruin would have been like going to a fine steakhouse and then ordering a hotdog. Melissa chose to stay behind. I asked her to keep an eye on the top of the ruin and made her promise that when I reached the top and raised my hands above my head, that she would take a picture.

I enthusiastically made my way to the base of the steps. Looking up at the ruin from the base made the trek up to the top appear to be much more of a chore than what it had appeared to be from a distance. I took a deep breath, gave myself a brief motivational speech, and proceeded to climb. As I made the trip to the top, I passed many who were sitting and trying to catch their breath. There were some people I met on the steps who had decided they had gone far enough and were not going to go all the way up, given the fact that it was far more physically daunting than they had thought. My legs were getting weak, I was sweating, and my conversations with others came to a stop in that I was too out of breath to speak. I had to focus. The steps were rugged, and there were no rails to help me keep my balance, and trust me, it was a long way down should someone lose their footing and fall. I kept my eye on the prize and was determined to reach my goal, and, not to mention, I was still very much a newlywed and had a bride at the base of the ruin to impress. I was not giving up.

I became emotional as my mind and heart suddenly realized the significance of what was taking place. This journey, up the ruin, had suddenly become much more than just climbing an ancient ruin for a photo to be taken. It had become a metaphor for what had transpired in my life over the past four years. My journey had not been easy, and it had been a journey with unimaginable obstacles. There had been some who stuck with me as I made my spiritual, emotional, and physical climb and others who had not. My journey, at times, had been accompanied by encouraging words from others, and, at times, my journey had been me and me alone.

My mind could not help from thinking about the many parallels between the ruins and myself. The Mayan structures were originally created to be something amazing, beautiful, and full of purpose. Abandoned and uncared for, they fell into a state of ruin and, as the lush vegetation of the jungle grew around them, they eventually became hidden from the world. With time, the ruins were rediscovered, and an urgent and careful campaign was started to restore the Mayan Ruins to their magnificent, original state.

That was me. I had been designed by God to be something extraordinary, and I let myself fall into a state of ruin. I, too, covered and hidden by a jungle of torment, was lost until life gave me a window of opportunity to put the past behind me. Despite my ruined state, God mercifully allowed me to rebuild a life of joy that is centered in Him. Through His ability to love and forgive, God extended to me a complete spiritual restoration while enthusiastically securing my place within His flock for all of eternity through the birth, life, death, and resurrection of His Son, Jesus Christ.

As I have taken steps forward and experienced so many blessings in my life, I know that it is God who has clearly given me the signs of my restoration and redemption. I am overwhelmed with gratitude as my heart and mind embrace what has transpired over the past several years. So many facets of my journey are viewed as miracles. Being a recipient of God's abundant grace and with Him having helped me rediscover the joy that can only be found through Christ, I want my story to be a source of hope and encouragement. My restoration and healing are a portrait of what God can do in the life of a sinner. My prayer is that others will learn to trust God and allow Him to fill the voids within their hearts and minds with His reassuring presence and unconditional love.

AFTERWORD

Melissa and I celebrate life daily. We choose to embrace and make the most of a life that will forever carry difficult memories and emotions. We know that our attitudes of joy and our intentional attempt to make the most of each day are a banner that we, together, want to hold high for others to see. Our home is our retreat. It is a haven to reflect on what we have learned is most important. We experience the joy of being surrounded by family, friends and by amazing brothers and sisters in Christ that provide for us a network of love and support. We approach each day knowing that God is in control and that His provisions for our lives go far beyond the needs and wants of this world. He has been faithful in keeping a watchful eye on our lives. We are mindful to reflect on what God has done for us in our journey as a couple and certainly in our spiritual walks with Him as individuals. God is amazing, and we have found that His promises are in place for all to enjoy no matter the sin, the circumstances, or situation.

Melissa knows my flaws, and yet, with heartfelt compassion, she is dedicated to me and the journey that we have entered together. My life is not easy. It, at times, continues to be a challenge to put my past behind me. I have days when my mind and heart are heavy with thoughts of what I did and the people I hurt. However, God continues to manage the pieces of my life and configure them in a way that is a portrait of a man who refuses to be defined by the mistakes he has made. God continues to convince me daily that I am of great value to Him. I have come to trust Him for the fatherly care and provisions I need in my life, and He has proven to me, time and time again, that He can be a mighty pillar of strength for me to lean upon in my times of doubt and discouragement.

I am grateful for those who have chosen to be a part of my journey and who continue to hold my hand as I take my steps carefully. I have discovered the joy of partnering with others in this, sometimes overwhelming, thing we call life. I rejoice in knowing that God remains faithful in His ability to restore each of us from a state of ruin into a life of redemption in, and through, His Son, Jesus Christ. Jesus loves me, this I know, and in Him, I have found my refuge.

ACKNOWLEDGMENTS

I am grateful for my wife, *Melissa*, who spent countless hours encouraging me as I wrote the pages of this book. She helped me to find the confidence to write the message of what God had placed on my heart. She is a source of inspiration and serves as a constant reminder that God is in control of every chapter of my life.

I am thankful for my friend, *Christina Murdock*. She provided valued guidance as I defined and wrote openly of the emotions that led to my fall. The direction and insight she provided in the writing and publication of this book was a treasured source of help as we took steps to complete this project.

My heartfelt gratitude to *Jason Jones* for providing advice throughout the editing process. His time, insight, and encouraging words were appreciated as I refined the pages of the book.

I would be remiss if I did not thank my colleague and friend, *Steve Cukovecki*, who has been a constant source of encouragement. On many days, he was the fuel that kept me ignited to complete this book.

Special thanks to:

Dale McCamish, Senior Minister of the Wilmington Church of Christ, Wilmington, Ohio

Drew Ireland, LPCC, Cincinnati, Ohio

The Ohio State Wexner Medical Center, Infectious Disease Staff, Columbus, Ohio